D1170757

A Culinary Palette

A Culinary Palette

Kitchen Masterpieces from Sixty-five Great Artists

Joan Mackie

Merritt Publishing Company Limited
Toronto/Vancouver

© 1981 Merritt Publishing Company Limited and
Joan Mackie

Published by Merritt Publishing Company Limited
Toronto/Vancouver

Distributed in Canada by John Wiley and Sons
Canada Limited

Canadian Cataloguing in Publication Data

Mackie, Joan.
  A culinary palette

Includes index.
ISBN 0-920886-11-6

1. Cookery. I. Title.

TX715.M32   641.5   C81-094565-7

Editor: Shelley Tanaka
Design: Frank Newfeld
Layout and assembly: Keith Abraham
Printed in the U.S.A.

For Victoria Robinson

Contents

List of Illustrations

Acknowledgements

Every author passes through several phases in writing a book and each phase has its own pleasures and excitement.

In my own case, the first phase, one of research, was more than pleasurable; it was a privilege. It brought me in touch with Christopher Youngs, director of the Canada Council Art Bank, who pointed me in many right directions, and with art historian Natalie Luckyj who helped me find just the right turn of phrase to describe the art work of some of the artists in the book.

This research phase, which took me across Canada—from a houseboat in British Columbia to a lighthouse in Newfoundland—gave me the opportunity to meet and become friends with numerous artists and their families, and with others in the art world. My life has been enriched by my association with these creative, friendly people, and it is with sincere gratitude that I thank them, not only for their enthusiastic contributions to the book, but also for welcoming me into their homes and their kitchens, and in some cases, their lives.

The second phase that the book and I passed through involved the testing of all the recipes. I don't know where most of them originated. Some sprang from the creative reserves of the artists themselves. I suspect too, that many were obtained from friends or culled from cookbooks. If I have printed a previously published recipe, I apologize for not being able to credit the source. I hope that the original author will be honoured by knowing that his or her recipe is in the repertoire of a creative artist and is thus in this book.

Testing the recipes, of course, meant tasting all the finished products. I was never at a loss for friends with sensitive palates who were willing and eager to sample and suggest during this phase of the book's development. I thank all of them for their sense of adventure, their patience, and their help.

I want also to give particularly warm and affectionate thanks to a very small group of friends who were especially close to me while I worked on the book. In the early stages, Hal Kalman supported and encouraged me, and joined me in tasting at least half the recipes. I thank him sincerely for his help. I give my special thanks, too, to Vicki and Glen Robinson, who were always available to assist and evaluate, and whose enthusiasm during the preparation of the book was delightfully infectious.

Whenever I was in need of any form of assistance, from recipe tasting to emergency shopping, no one was more willing than Janice Sonnen. I thank her for this, as well as for her skill in knowing when and how to dispense appropriate measures of reassurance and encouragement. I also thank Larry Ryan who was an eager *sous chef* whenever he was in town, and Ivan Chorney who both cooked and sampled with me, and then insisted I sit at my typewriter when deadlines loomed and other temptations beckoned.

I have many reasons for thanking my architect and friend, Keith Wagland, but mostly I thank him for designing for me the kitchen in which I happily tested most of the recipes in the book.

Finally, I give my thanks to artist Jerry Grey, who is in this book, and who in a sense is responsible for it. It was she who more than a decade ago called my attention to the fact that cooking is a form of artistic expression no less important than the sculpture of a sculptor or the painting of a painter. Jerry Grey opened my eyes to this concept, paving the way for this book.

Introduction

Dinner guests at the home of artist Francis Coutellier never need to dodge a traditional flowers-and-candelabra centrepiece in order to talk across the table. They may, however, find themselves separated by one of his works of art. Once it was a large bulging beef heart. Garnished appropriately, cooked to perfection, it seemed to be pulsating with life. On another occasion, colourful jellies in fanciful shapes decorated the table. So tempting were they, though, that by the end of the evening, the guests had devoured all of their host's creations. Does it seem strange that an artist should have this close affinity with food? It shouldn't.

History is studded with examples of the association that exists between the visual and the culinary arts. Sixteenth-century artist Andrea del Sarto often worked with food. Influenced by the architecture of the period, he once created an edible baptistry from sausages, cheese, marzipan, and lasagna. His teacher, Italian Renaissance painter Piero di Cosimo, whose diet consisted of hard-boiled eggs, habitually cooked them fifty at a time in the glue he was boiling for his canvases.

It took the flowering of the seventeenth century to elevate food to an artistic level—both in the kitchen and on canvas. Artists were no longer limited to producing art for religious or royal purposes. The Baroque painters Jan Davidsz. de Heem, Willem Claesz. Heda, and their contemporaries depicted luscious mouth-watering still-lifes, many of which hang in major art galleries today.

In the eighteenth century, wood engravings became popular, and many showed scenes of frantic kitchen activity. It was during this century, too, that cookery books appeared, for more than "select" households, often illustrated with typically rococo decorations.

In France, Marie-Antoine Carême, the late-eighteenth-century Paris-born *chef extraordinaire*, elevated cooking to an art form. Art stimulated his culinary creativity and he spent years at the Imperial Library and Cabinet of Engravings perfecting his drawing technique (which he transferred to his culinary works), inspired by the art sources he found there. In his memoirs, he says:

> I was a pastry cook at Bailly's. . . . He gave me time off to study designs from prints. . . . My ambition was serious and at an early age I became desirous of elevating my profession to an art. . . . [In art and in cooking] the manner is comparable in which the artist sets out his colours on the palette in the same way that a chef enriches a sauce and measures his seasonings.

By the nineteenth century, food as subject matter for art was firmly established. Impressionist painters such as Manet, Renoir, and Degas all painted scenes in which food was one of the elements.

Toulouse-Lautrec and Gauguin were both known to have thanked their dinner hostesses by sending them delicate portrait-sketches, embellished with drawings of the foods they had been served. And at the turn of this century, when illustrated menus by great artists were not uncommon, James Ensor, Belgian contemporary of Gauguin, once drew a menu of the wedding feast that celebrated the marriage of his close friend, Ernest Rousseau. A copy was made for each of the guests to take home as a memento.

Down through the centuries, food themes have repeatedly appeared in paintings: fruits and vegetables, fish and wine, banqueting feasts, pastoral picnics, and market scenes. Artists continually draw on food sources for inspiration in their work; similarly art stimulates culinary creativity.

In England, restaurant owner Peter Langan provides his customers with menus drawn by pop-artist David Hockney. In the United States what better known contemporary works of art are there than Claes Oldenburg's *Giant Hamburger* or Andy Warhol's Campbells Soup series?

And in Canada? From the ceramic foods of Vancouver's Gathie Falk to the acrylic fish and jam jars of Newfoundland's Mary Pratt, there are hundreds of works of art inspired by food sources being created by artists scattered throughout all the provinces.

Vancouver artist Iain Baxter successfully married the visual and the culinary arts in his Eye Scream Restaurant, which he described as "a big piece of sculpture." Patrons dined on Steak Salvador Dali and Scallops Renoir, surrounded by paintings, sculpture, and ever-changing art exhibits.

Nova Scotian John Greer frequently uses food themes as his *Spoon Fed Culture* on page 104 shows. A glance through the catalogue of one of his recent exhibitions at the Dalhousie Art Gallery turns up such titles as *Oranges of Canadian Art (for Dennis Reid), Three Geese Disguised,* and *The Proverbial Grain of Salt.*

Famous for her culinary skills, Toronto artist Rita Letendre was invited to participate in a gala fund-raising dinner. For the event, the "Celebrity Chefs' Cooking Ball," she created the main course—a sunburst of orange-glazed rock Cornish game hens radiating from a mound of herbed bulghur. It was a veritable work of art.

In the summer of 1978, Bruce Parsons expected to spend two weeks in rural Newfoundland at the St. Michael's Printshop, leading a workshop which the brochures described as "a two-week experience in drawing, painting, printmaking, sculpture, and photography using a seaside and woodland environment." Quite by accident, the workshop developed into a two-week experience in culinary creativity, inspired by the bounty of the neighbouring land and sea. The works of art that resulted from this shift in interest very much reflected an unleashed passion for food!

Few though these examples may be, I cite them merely to tempt further exploration into the enjoyment that results from the relationship between food, art, and artists. This book documents, for the first time, the connection between the visual and the culinary arts in Canada.

I hope it will permit those who appreciate the visual arts to see contemporary artists from a new perspective, their creativity in food. I hope, too, that those who appreciate the culinary arts will, perhaps as never before, be able to combine this pleasure with a new appreciation of the visual arts. Most important of all, I hope this cookbook will be treasured as a collection of new—and superb—recipes from the kitchens of some of the most creative cooks in Canada.

Marcel Barbeau

During the first six months of Marcel and Ninon Barbeau's marriage, Marcel did all the cooking. "He was very good," Ninon says, "and I let him — perhaps I was just being lazy. But eventually I couldn't keep quiet any longer. I had to tell him that I came from a long line of accomplished cooks."

What a surprise it was to Marcel, for soon the table was set with Ninon's specialties from the Charlevoix region of Quebec where she was raised. Marcel was not, however, entirely displaced. Over the years, things have evened out to the point where they combine their culinary skills and work together in the kitchen, often in the preparation of the same dish.

"Marcel taught me a lot of things I didn't know," she laughs, "including how to make wonderful *moules marinières* and how to gather and prepare wild mushrooms."

"When we're at our summer farm-home in St-Irénée (a small village on the north shore of the St. Lawrence River, near Quebec City) we collect *chanterelles* and *cèpes* very early in the day, just when they're opening. The timing is very important," says Marcel.

"We like to slice them thin and fry them with a little minced onion in a pan that has just cooked some diced bacon. When they're well sautéed, we add some chopped parsley, chives, and tarragon, the bacon, perhaps a little cream, and there it is.

"At our St-Irénée farm, eating is such a delight because we have access to so many good foods. A neighbouring relative also has a farm so we can have all the fresh vegetables we want and the nearby rivers and streams are full of trout. I take time out from my painting and in a morning I can easily catch six or eight of them, which we prepare for lunch. To prepare them, I just shake them in a bag of flour and herbs, and pan fry in a little butter. Occasionally, if I've caught a lot, we'll make some trout pâté."

Considering Marcel's background, it is remarkable that he is such an accomplished cook. "My mother wouldn't let me help in the kitchen when I was a child, because traditionally, only the girls were expected to cook and I had three sisters," he says. "However, when I got out on my own, I realized my ambition to create wonderful things with food.

"Ninon and I like to harmonize food as if it were a symphony. Anything one eats must be well presented. The eye is very important in an appreciation of food."

Marcel's Omelette

3 slices	bacon, cut in small pieces
1 Tbsp (15mL)	butter
2	small onions, finely diced
1 cup (250mL)	small croutons
5	eggs
¼ cup (50mL)	water
1 Tbsp (15mL)	cognac
½ tsp (2mL)	dry mustard
	salt and pepper
4 leaves	fresh tarragon, finely minced

Heat a heavy frying pan. Sauté bacon until crisp. Remove from pan with a slotted spoon. Pour off all but 1 table-spoon (15mL) fat. Add butter. Sauté onion until transparent. Return bacon to frying pan and add croutons. Distribute evenly.

Beat eggs with water, cognac, mustard, salt, pepper, and minced tarragon. Pour into frying pan. Cook for 3 minutes over medium heat, shaking pan occasionally and lifting edges of cooked egg so liquid will run underneath. Cook until set. Broil close to heat until golden.

Serves 4

Soupe aux gourganes
Broad Bean Soup

6 cups (1.5L)	water
½ pound (250g)	salt pork
1	whole large onion
1	*bouquet garni* (savory, chervil, parsley, and marjoram, tied together in cheesecloth)
1 pound (500g)	broad beans
1	carrot, coarsely diced in ½-inch (1-cm) cubes
1	large onion, finely diced
¼	turnip, coarsely diced in ½-inch (1-cm) cubes
¼ pound (125g)	yellow beans, finely diced
¼ cup (50mL)	barley
4	young leaves of turnip
1	egg yolk
⅓ cup (75mL)	cream
3 sprigs	parsley, finely chopped
3 sprigs	chervil, finely chopped
3 sprigs	savory, finely chopped
	croutons, as garnish

Combine water, salt pork, whole onion, and *bouquet garni* in a large saucepan. Cover and simmer for 1 hour. While this is cooking, take a sharp knife and remove the outer skins from the broad beans.

At the end of the cooking time, remove the salt pork, onion, and *bouquet garni* from the stock. Add vegetables, including beans, and barley. Cover and simmer for 30 minutes.

Cut turnip leaves in narrow strips and add to soup. Cook for 5 minutes.

In a small bowl, beat egg yolk with cream and finely chopped herbs. Stir in a few spoonfuls of soup to heat the egg. Then slowly pour the egg mixture into the soup, stirring constantly. Heat through but do not allow to boil.

Serve garnished with croutons.

Serves 10

Chaland d'éperlans à la mode de St-Irénée
Smelt Pie, St. Irénée-style

	Crust
1⅓ cups (325mL)	flour
dash of	salt
¼ tsp (1mL)	baking powder
⅓ cup (75mL)	unsalted butter
3 Tbsp (40mL)	ice water

	Filling
2 dozen	fresh smelts
2	onions, finely minced
¼ cup (50mL)	minced parsley
¼ cup (50mL)	minced chives
1 cup (250mL)	minced sorrel
2 tsp (10mL)	minced savory
1 Tbsp (15mL)	butter
	salt and pepper
¼ cup (50mL)	cream
1	egg yolk
2 tsp (10mL)	flour
2 tsp (10mL)	butter

To make the crust, sift together the flour, salt, and baking powder. With a pastry cutter or two knives, cut in the butter until the mixture has the texture of coarse meal. Toss with enough water to hold dough together and form into a ball. Roll out in 2 pieces, fitting a deep, 8-inch (1-L) pie pan with the larger piece and saving the smaller one for the top crust.

To make the filling, clean the fish and fillet them by removing the head and fins with scissors. Slash the back from tail to head with a sharp knife, and lift out the bone and rib cage. Refrigerate until ready to use.

Combine minced onion and minced herbs. Sauté in butter until soft. Spread one-third of this mixture in the pie shell. Cover with half the smelts. Season with salt and pepper. Cover with another third of the onion and herb mixture and the remaining smelts. Sprinkle with salt and pepper. Top with remaining herb and onion mixture.

Combine cream, egg yolk, and flour. Reserve 1 tablespoon (15mL) and pour remaining egg mixture into pie. Dot with butter. Cover with the top pie crust. Moisten edges and crimp to seal. Cut air vents in pastry. Brush with reserved cream and egg mixture. Bake at 350°F (180°C) for 35 minutes.

Serves 4

Mousse aux framboises
Raspberry Mousse

2 cups (500mL)	raspberries
2	egg whites
pinch of	cream of tartar
1 tsp (5mL)	lemon juice
¾ cup (175mL)	powdered fruit sugar
2 Tbsp (25mL)	kirsch

Purée raspberries in a blender. Force through a fine sieve.

Beat egg whites with cream of tartar until stiff peaks form, gradually adding lemon juice and sugar. Fold in raspberry purée and kirsch.

Spoon into individual serving dishes or a large serving bowl. Chill for at least 1 hour before serving.

Serves 6

Tarte nicharageoise
Blueberry and Peach Pie

Pastry
1 cup (250mL)	flour
¼ cup (50mL)	sugar
pinch of	salt
pinch of	baking powder
2 Tbsp (25mL)	unsalted butter
2	egg yolks
2 Tbsp (25mL)	cold water
¼ tsp (1mL)	orange flower water

Crème pâtissière
1 Tbsp (15mL)	flour
½ cup (125mL)	sugar
3	egg yolks
1¼ cups (300mL)	warm milk
½ tsp (2mL)	orange flower water

Fruits and Syrup
1 cup (250mL)	water
1 cup (250mL)	sugar
2 cups (500mL)	blueberries
3	peaches, sliced

Glaze
½ cup (125mL)	fruit syrup
1 Tbsp (15mL)	red currant jelly
1 Tbsp (15mL)	cornstarch, dissolved in 2 Tbsp (25mL) water

To make the pastry, sift together the dry ingredients. Cut in the butter using a pastry blender or 2 knives, until the mixture has the consistency of coarse meal. Combine egg yolks, water, and orange flower water. Toss with flour and combine to form a stiff dough. Add a little more water if necessary to form a ball. Chill for 1 hour. Roll out to fit the bottom and sides of a 9-inch (1-L) flan pan with removable sides. Bake at 350°F (180°C) for 20 to 25 minutes or until golden.

To make the *crème pâtissière*, combine the flour and sugar in the top of a double boiler set over hot water. Add egg yolks and with an electric mixer, beat until eggs become light in colour. Slowly add warm milk and orange flower water. Cook, stirring constantly, until mixture thickens. Remove from heat and let cool, stirring occasionally. Pour into baked crust.

To make the syrup, combine the water and sugar. Divide in half. In one half, poach the blueberries for 2 minutes. In the other half, poach the peach slices for 5 minutes. Strain the syrup from both fruits and reserve that in which the peaches were poached.

Mentally dividing the pie in quarters, spread blueberry topping in wedges opposite each other, and peach topping on the other opposing quarters.

Measure ½ cup (125mL) of the reserved syrup. Heat it with red currant jelly and dissolved cornstarch until thickened. Use to glaze pie. Allow to stand for 3 hours before serving. Remove sides from pan before serving.

Serves 8

Iain Baxter, President, N.E. THING CO., *An open-face sandwich*, 1977. Hand-tinted photowork, 13 cm × 19 cm. Collection of the Canada Council Art Bank. Photo: Yvan Boulerice.

Iain Baxter/N.E. THING CO.

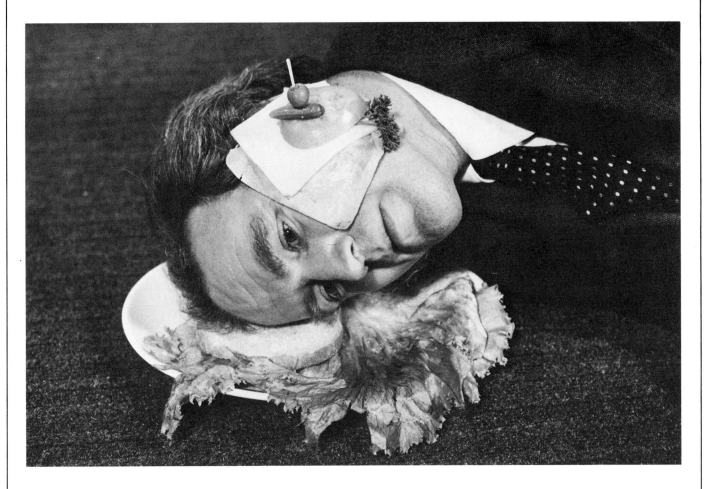

"I'm working on developing a repertoire of off-beat recipes," says Iain Baxter, president of N.E. THING CO. This, as many people know, is the company through which Iain Baxter produces his multi-faceted artistic endeavours — gallery exhibits, "happenings," books, and for a couple of years in the late seventies, an innovative Vancouver restaurant called Eye Scream, which Iain described as "a big piece of sculpture." Located on a busy Kitsilano street, the building was the jewel of the block, its shiny metal and mirror exterior sparkling in the glare of the sun or streetlights.

Part art gallery, part restaurant, Eye Scream was a place where all the senses were stimulated. The palate was tempted by Steak Salvador Dali and Scallops Renoir. The eye would dart from the walls to the ceiling to the floor — all decorated with ever-changing and often mobile exhibits; the ear was challenged by live musicians. Lest one be confused by the cacophony, the chinaware was all stamped with the name of the piece in art deco block lettering: CUP, SAUCER, BOWL, PLATE.

Obviously, Iain enjoys playing with food — and in many ways. Having buttered a large piece of bread, and cradling it on a lettuce leaf, he laid his head on it, topped off with a slice each of ham, cheese, and tomato. Then he called in the photographer, and *voilà*, the finished product: an art work, *An open-face sandwich*.

While Iain claims not to be much of a cook, he has many ideas about food and cooking. There's no doubt, however, that for him, food is an art form, and he constantly exploits the connection between the visual and the culinary arts.

White Lightning

1 cup (250mL)	milk
2 ounces (50mL)	Grand Marnier or favourite liqueur
	freshly grated nutmeg

Heat milk but do not allow to boil. Pour liqueur into a heated glass and slowly add hot milk. Top with grated nutmeg.

Serves 1

Tacos in a Bowl or Hot Salad

4	tomatoes, each cut into eight wedges
4	avocados, sliced
6 bunches	green onions, sliced
2 heads	lettuce, shredded
5	green peppers, sliced
2 8-ounce (250-g)	bags taco chips
1½ pounds (750g)	grated Cheddar cheese
2 Tbsp (25mL)	vegetable oil
2 pounds (1kg)	ground beef
1	garlic clove, crushed
3 14-ounce (398-mL)	cans kidney beans, drained
2 14-ounce (398-mL)	cans tomato sauce

Prepare vegetables as indicated and set each kind in a separate bowl. Pile the taco chips and grated cheese in separate bowls also.

Heat oil in a large frying pan. Add ground beef and sauté until brown. Pour off excess fat. Stir in the garlic, kidney beans, and tomato sauce. Simmer, covered, for 30 minutes, stirring occasionally. Transfer to a hot serving dish.

To serve, set the bowls on a table in the following order: taco chips, vegetables, meat mixture, grated cheese. Guests will layer their own salad bowls in this order.

Serves 8

Quick Pseudo-Caesar Salad with Spinach

2 10-ounce (283-g)	packages spinach
4	tomatoes, cut in wedges
2	avocados, sliced
1 bunch	green onions, chopped
½ pound (250g)	mushrooms, sliced
half a	can of anchovies, finely chopped
1	egg
¾ cup (175mL)	oil and vinegar dressing (approx.)
	juice of half a lemon
dash of	Worcestershire sauce
	salt and pepper

Wash spinach, discarding tough stems and blemished leaves. Dry thoroughly. Toss with tomatoes, avocados, green onions, mushrooms, and anchovies.

Break the egg into a 2-cup (500-mL) measure. Pour in enough dressing to raise level to 1 cup (250mL). Add lemon juice and Worcestershire sauce and beat together with a fork or small whisk.

Just before serving, toss the salad with salt, pepper, and the dressing.

Serves 8

Scrambled Eggs with Anchovies

8	eggs
2 Tbsp (25mL)	milk
2 Tbsp (25mL)	commercial sour cream
4	anchovies, finely chopped
¼ cup (50mL)	chopped parsley
2 Tbsp (25mL)	butter

Beat eggs lightly with milk and sour cream. Add chopped anchovies and parsley.

Melt butter in a medium-sized frying pan and pour in eggs. Stir constantly over medium heat until eggs are scrambled — firm yet moist.

Serve on toast.

Serves 4

Derek Besant and Alexandra Haeseker

"I like a pie that fights back," declares Derek Besant, which is probably the reason his wife's Saskatoonberry pie is such a favourite.

"Mixing whole wheat with regular pastry flour gives the crust a more interesting flavour," says Sandy Haeseker, "and using less sugar for the filling than is called for in most recipes makes the unique taste of the berries more obvious."

Derek and Sandy, who both teach at the Alberta College of Art, live on a Saskatoonberry-covered farm south of Calgary, near the town of Okotoks. Whoever arrives home first gets the meals ready.

They have widely different culinary backgrounds, so there is a lot of variety in their meals. Derek grew up in southern Alberta where good, solid Canadian food was served and enjoyed. Sandy was born in Holland, of parents who had been raised in the Netherlands East Indies. She came to Canada at the age of ten, but remembers vividly the Indonesian food of her childhood, and today enjoys cooking and experimenting with that cuisine.

Parties at their home are often "evenings of decadence," says Derek, "when Sandy makes Nasi Goreng Één Twee Drie."

"It's the type of meal where anything goes," Sandy explains. "The more flavour and texture combinations, the better the meal becomes. Derek and I have given the meal — adapted from inventions of my family — this special name. It's a mixture of Malayan and Dutch and translated means 'fried rice ready in a jiffy.' "

Because they like to cook together, they often pool talents and mix cuisines if a party is planned. Derek's mother has been immortalized in Laura's Lima Beans — a party favourite because it is easily doubled or tripled.

Derek also claims to make an irresistible spinach salad. "We have a small garden that's big on wildlife — about four acres — but it hasn't been too successful," admits Derek. "Our spinach grew like crazy and got really big, then one night it slunk back down into the ground. I think it was too close to the forest."

19

Kroketjes den Haag
Croquettes the Hague

3 Tbsp (40mL)	butter or margarine
4 Tbsp (50mL)	flour
1 cup (250mL)	hot beef stock
½ tsp (2mL)	lemon juice
¼ tsp (1mL)	pepper
1½ cups (375mL)	chopped cooked meat (beef or chicken)
1	egg white, lightly beaten
2 cups (500mL)	Paneermeel or ground Dutch rusks (approx.)
	oil for deep frying

Melt butter in the top of a double boiler. Stir in flour, then gradually add hot stock. Cook over boiling water until mixture thickens, stirring constantly. Add lemon juice, pepper, and chopped meat. Combine thoroughly and spread mixture on a plate, about ¼ inch (5mm) thick. Chill for 2 hours to stiffen.

Divide mixture into 12 equal portions and roll each into the shape of a sausage. Roll in Paneermeel or rusk crumbs, coating evenly. Dip in beaten egg white, then roll again in Paneermeel. Heat oil at least 2 inches (5cm) deep to 385°F (195°C.) Lower kroketjes into hot oil and fry until golden brown — about 4 minutes. Remove with a slotted spoon and drain on paper towels before serving.

Traditionally, in the Netherlands, kroketjes are split down the middle and served on a slice of bread, then eaten with a knife and fork.

Yield: 12 kroketjes

Nasi Goreng Één Twee Drie

1 ounce (30g)	Boemboe Nasi Goreng (dehydrated vegetables and spices, e.g. Conimex brand, available in Dutch specialty stores)
¼ cup (50mL)	boiling water
2 Tbsp (25mL)	vegetable oil
6 cups (1.5L)	cooked rice
7-ounce (200-g)	can corned beef, crumbled

Put Boemboe Nasi Goreng in a small bowl. Cover with boiling water and let steep for 15 minutes. Drain off water. Heat oil in a wok or large frying pan. Stir in Boemboe Nasi Goreng and fry for 1 to 2 minutes. Add cooked rice and crumbled corned beef. Heat through, stirring constantly, for about 10 minutes.

This is a main dish which may be served with the following condiments:

Pisang Goreng (Fried Banana)
Cut 2 bananas in half and split lengthwise into 8 pieces. Fry in a little oil over moderate heat until bananas are soft and brown.

Sambal Corn Flakes
Put 1 tablespoon (15mL) vegetable oil and 2 teaspoons (10mL) Sambal Oelek in a large frying pan. Add 4 cups (1L) corn flakes and ½ cup (125mL) brown sugar and fry lightly, stirring constantly for 3 to 5 minutes.

Cucumber Slices and Sambal
Peel 1 cucumber and cut into thin slices. Chop ¼ cup (50mL) green onion. Combine in a small bowl and cover with white vinegar to which has been added 1 teaspoon (5mL) Sambal Oelek. Chill.

Tomato in Ketjap
Slice 2 tomatoes, place in a bowl, and cover with Ketjap Bentang Manis.

Traditionally, Nasi Goreng is eaten from a deep bowl with a fork and spoon. The main rice dish is placed in a mound in the middle, allowing room to add the various side dishes. A fried egg can be laid on top and then sprinkled with Sambal Corn Flakes and peanuts. All ingredients may be found in specialty food stores.

Serves 4

Derek Besant, *Spill Life #6,* 1976. Watercolour and ink
on rag paper, 33 cm × 38.1 cm. Collection of Mr.
and Mrs. Jon S. Sigurdson, Vancouver. Photo: Mira
Godard Gallery, Toronto.

Laura's Lima Beans (Bar-B-Q Style)

2 cups (500mL)	dried lima beans
1 quart (1L)	water
¼ pound (125g)	salt pork, cut in 4 pieces
1	onion, chopped
1	garlic clove, crushed
¼ cup (50mL)	vegetable oil
1 10-ounce (284-mL)	can undiluted tomato soup
2 tsp (10mL)	Worcestershire sauce
1½ Tbsp (25mL)	prepared mustard
1 Tbsp (15mL)	chili powder
¼ cup (50mL)	white vinegar
1 tsp (5mL)	salt
¼ pound (125g)	back bacon, chopped

Rinse beans well under running cold water. Soak them overnight in 1 quart (1L) water.

Add salt pork to beans. Bring to a boil, reduce heat, and simmer until beans are soft — about 2 hours. Drain off liquid and reserve. Discard salt pork. Set beans aside.

Brown onion and garlic in oil.

Pour tomato soup into a large ovenproof casserole. Combine with 1 cup (250mL) reserved liquid. Add Worcestershire sauce, mustard, chili powder, vinegar, and salt. Stir in beans, onion, garlic, and back bacon. Bake uncovered at 350°(F) 180°C for 1 hour.

Serves 3 to 4

Okotoks Saskatoonberry Pie

Pastry

1 cup (250mL)	whole wheat flour
1½ cups (375mL)	pastry flour
1 tsp (5mL)	salt
½ cup (125mL)	shortening
⅓ cup (75mL)	cold water (approx.)

Filling

1 quart (1L)	Saskatoonberries, washed and picked over
⅓ cup (75mL)	granulated sugar
2 Tbsp (25mL)	flour
1 tsp (5mL)	lemon juice

Make pastry by sifting together the whole wheat flour, pastry flour, and salt. With a pastry cutter or two knives, cut in shortening until mixture resembles coarse meal. Tossing with a fork, gradually add enough water to hold ingredients together to form a ball. Divide dough in half, wrap each piece in waxed paper, and chill for 30 minutes.

Roll out half the dough into a circle about ⅛ inch (2mm) thick. Fit into a 9-inch (1-L) pie plate. Fill with berries. Sprinkle with sugar, flour, and lemon juice.

Roll out remaining dough into a circle that is ⅛ inch (2mm) thick. Place on top of berries. Trim to fit. Moisten edges with water. Crimp together with the tines of a fork. Cut steam vents in top crust. Brush with beaten egg or cream. Bake at 425°F (220°C) for 40 minutes.

Alexandra Haeseker, *Porklift,* 1976. Print, 75.5 cm × 56 cm. Photo: Don Nicolson Photography, courtesy of the Art Gallery of Brant.

Porklift   3/40   Alexandra Haeseker '76

André Biéler

André Biéler comes from a tradition in which "men were never found in the kitchen," his wife Jeannette says, but he seems to function very well in one when necessary.

During a recent summer, he and two friends spent a week on a houseboat, cruising up the Rideau Canal from his Kingston home. His main reason for organizing the trip was to paint the landscape along the canal, but his friend, historian Arthur Lower, who was responsible for the cleaning up, said that André did a superb job of planning and cooking the meals.

"I can see the possibilities in things, but I'm not really a cook," André says. "On the boat, I occasionally found myself in despair. We craved onions but had none. So we phoned a friend and invited him on board — as long as he brought a bag of onions. They were so good — I fried them with ham slices. I also did some superb chicken fried in olive oil and glazed with soy sauce. It came out all shiny black."

André Biéler sees a strong connection between the visual and the culinary arts and theorizes that the struggling, impecunious artist in his garret studio could economize by using cooking ingredients for painting.

"His baking flour could be used for the pigment in his paintings. His milk, eggs, oil, and gelatin could all be used as adhesives in his pigments. His sugar could be mixed with a waxy substance and used for etching, and his bread could be used for cleaning his watercolours."

Fortunately for André, he need not live the life of his imaginary struggling artist; he enjoys the best in food. And while he may not spend a lot of time in the kitchen, he has some sound principles that any cook would do well to heed.

"Your materials must be of first quality and very fresh. So you should read the grocery ads in the newspaper and not buy anything that is advertised. They want to get rid of it, you see, that's why they put it on special. You never see olive oil on sale, now, do you?"

Summer Garden Vegetables

2 Tbsp (25mL)	olive oil
1	onion, chopped
5	zucchini, cut in ¼-inch (5-mm) thick rounds
2	tomatoes, cut in wedges, seeds removed
1	green pepper, cut in chunks
½ pound (250g)	mushrooms, sliced
1	garlic clove, crushed
1 Tbsp (15mL)	fresh tarragon, or ½ tsp (2mL) dried tarragon
1 Tbsp (15mL)	fresh basil, or ½ tsp (2mL) dried basil
½ tsp (2mL)	salt
	freshly ground pepper
¼ cup (50mL)	crumbled shredded wheat

Heat oil in a large frying pan. Sauté the onion until golden. Add zucchini, tomatoes, green pepper, mushrooms, and garlic. Stir over medium heat until vegetables are cooked but still *al dente* (tender yet firm). Towards the end of the cooking time, add the herbs.

Serve while very hot, sprinkled with crumbled shredded wheat.

Serves 4

André Biéler, *Still Life*, 1980. Pen and ink on card, 11 cm × 12 cm.

Ronald Bloore

Toronto painter Ron Bloore, who thinks he may have the largest private collection of wooden spoons in Canada, never uses them for the purposes for which they were intended. Instead, he arranges them into artistic sculptures.

Ron Bloore has only one recipe in his repertoire. He says he doesn't have the time to cook and admits that he is not really interested in cooking either. "I eat out almost all the time. I don't really care what I eat as long as I feel full."

Ron and his wife, art connoisseur Dorothy Cameron, are both busy people who seldom eat at home. "I like lots of junk food," he says.

"At home, I love Sara Lee cakes because you don't have to do anything to them except eat them. And if I find myself hungry, I might make a ketchup sandwich, which I think is delicious. Did you know that I once worked in a ketchup plant?"

Bloorewich

Heinz ketchup on white bread, no butter, folded over.

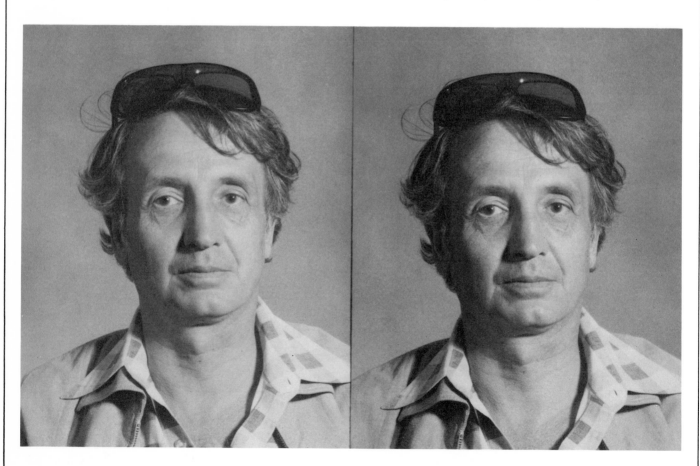

Ronald Bloore, *The Table,* 1975. Set piece. Reproduced from *artscanada,* June, 1975, "The Artist as Historian." Photo: Eberhard Otto.

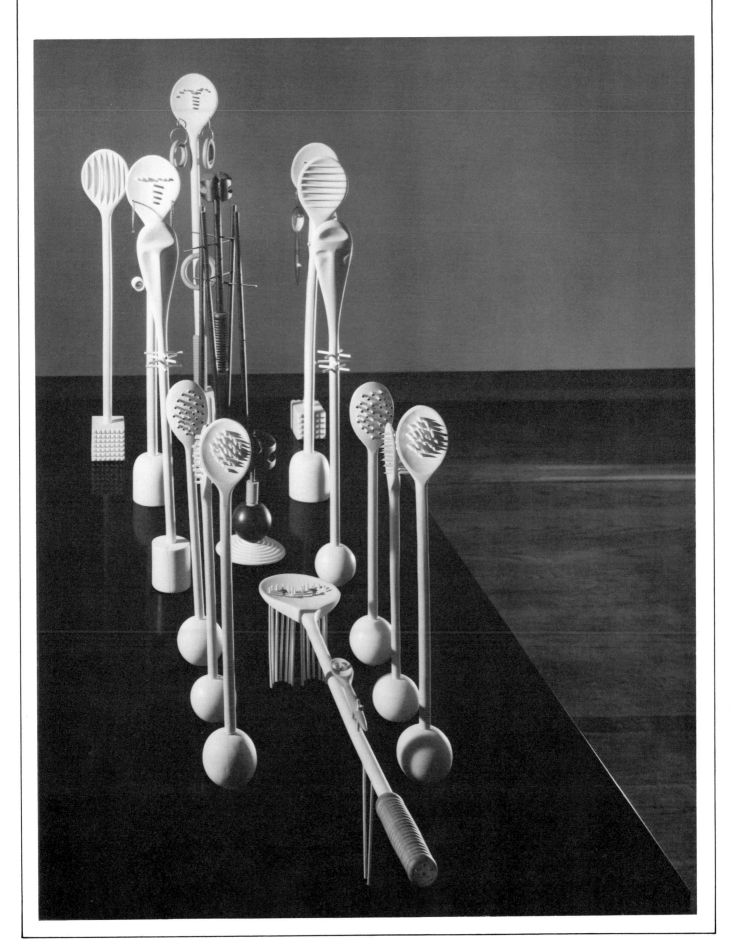

André Biéler, *Quelques Coqs,* 1979. Gold leaf on gesso,
183 cm × 234 cm. Collection of the artist. Photo:
Gerry Locklin.

Bruno Bobak and Molly Lamb Bobak

Bruno Bobak and Molly Lamb Bobak are two Canadian painters who work in very different styles. Both are very good cooks too, but as in their art, they bring distinctive touches to their culinary specialties.

"I'm a slow-stove cook," says Molly, "and I think really that my stove does all the work for me. In the winter, I make long slow things like oxtail stew, which is left in the oven all day." Bruno also says that she's "great on soups and pies — especially rhubarb, picked from our garden."

Since 1962, the Bobaks have lived in Fredericton where Bruno is director of the University of New Brunswick Art Centre. They met when both worked as official war artists for the Canadian government.

Behind their charming old home is an enormous vegetable garden that produces, in addition to the rhubarb, eight-foot high peas and leeks that last all through the winter.

Bruno is a bass fiend and keeps a boat on top of his car so he can put it into the St. John River whenever he feels the urge to fish. He and his friend Jimmy Pataki, a musician with the Brunswick String Quartet, caught more than four hundred bass during the summer of 1978, and over five hundred the following year.

"At first, we used to fish for anything — pickerel, perch, even chub — until we discovered a bass hole. We were excited by the fighting spirit of the bass and even more surprised by the taste of the fish. The flesh is firm, sweet, juicy, and practically boneless when filleted. I'm not knocking salmon, but I actually prefer bass.

"We have a certain ritual with bass fishing — we each take a bottle of wine to quench our thirst. We used to take our home-made wine, but we couldn't brew fast enough to keep up with our fishing trips. The wine is a very important part of our ritual because we toast ourselves for the flimsiest reasons. We start with a 'preparatory' drink, and, of course, we have a 'congratulatory' drink for catching a fish, and we have a 'consolatory' drink when a fish gets away. We even have a 'suppository' drink for when one of

Photo: Marc Sabat

Photo: Ian Brown

us behaves like an asshole, like once when Jimmy threw a whole string of fish overboard.

"After a couple of hours of fishing, we come home, mellow from the wine, to continue our ritual, which is cleaning the fish. With a glass of scotch and water, we settle ourselves down at the patio table with lots of newspaper and wasps and pussy cats. The large fish we scale and clean — they're great for baking — the rest we just fillet and throw in the freezer."

Slow-stove Bread

1 cup (250mL)	lukewarm water
¼ cup (50mL)	granulated sugar
2 packages	yeast
1 cup (250mL)	white flour
2½ cups (625mL)	water mixed with ⅓ cup (75mL) milk powder
½ cup (125mL)	of each of the following: oatmeal, flax seed, kasha, poppy seed, sesame seed, millet, and bran
5½ cups (1.25L)	whole wheat flour plus 1 cup (250mL) flour to use during kneading (approx.)
2 tsp (10mL)	salt

In a medium-sized bowl, place 1 cup (250mL) water, granulated sugar, and yeast. Let stand for ten minutes.

Meanwhile, place 1 cup (250mL) white flour in a large bowl. Gradually add water and powdered milk mixture. Stir in the yeast mixture and the grains.

Add 5½ cups (1.25L) whole wheat flour and salt, stirring until dough is too stiff to handle. Then turn out onto a board floured with remaining 1 cup (250mL) flour and knead until smooth and elastic — about 10 minutes.

Divide into 2 balls and knead each ball for a further 2 or 3 minutes. Shape into loaves and place in 2 greased bread pans, cover with a clean towel, and set to rise in a warm, draft-free place until the dough has risen above the sides of the pans — about 1 to 1½ hours.

Bake at 325°F (160°C) for about 50 minutes. Turn out of pans and cool on a wire rack.

Yield: 2 loaves

Baked Bass

4	small bass
2 cups (500mL)	poultry stuffing (approx.)
	butter

Clean and wash bass. Remove gills. Stuff the cavities with favourite poultry stuffing. Sew up opening or secure with skewers. Place on greased baking pan. Dot with butter. Bake at 400°F (200°C) for 20 minutes.

Serves 4

Bass Soup

2 pounds (1kg)	bass fillets
2 tsp (10mL)	salt
	freshly ground pepper
	juice of 1 lemon
½ tsp (2mL)	Hungarian sweet paprika
2	bay leaves
2	carrots, diced
3	large onions, sliced
2	stalks celery, diced
6	potatoes, diced
2 quarts (2L)	water

Cut the fish into bite-sized pieces. Sprinkle with salt and pepper. Cover with lemon juice and set aside for 1 hour.

Combine remaining ingredients in a large saucepan. Simmer, covered, for 1 hour.

Drain the fish and add to the vegetables. Simmer for 15 minutes. Add salt and pepper to taste.

Serves 8

Grilled Bass

4	small bass, cleaned, or 8 bass fillets
½ cup (125mL)	vegetable oil
½ cup (125mL)	flour
4	lemon wedges, as garnish

Brush bass with vegetable oil and sprinkle with flour. Place fish in a hinged grill and cook over hot coals in a hibachi or barbecue for about 5 minutes per side. Brush frequently with oil during cooking. Bass is cooked when it flakes easily but is still moist.

Serve with lemon wedges.

Serves 4

Bruno Bobak, *Bass,* 1978. Charcoal on paper, 11.4 cm
× 20.4 cm. Collection of Keith H. Wagland, Toronto.

Baked Eel or Bass Fillets

2 pounds (1kg)	skinned eel or bass fillets
2 tsp (10mL)	salt
	freshly ground pepper
	juice of 1 lemon
3	eggs
2 Tbsp (25mL)	water
2 cups (500mL)	fresh bread crumbs
½ cup (125mL)	melted butter

Sprinkle fish with salt and pepper. Cover with lemon juice and set aside for 1 hour. Drain and dry well with paper towels.

Beat eggs with water. Dip fish fillets alternately in egg and bread crumbs several times. Arrange a single layer of fillets in a round buttered ovenproof dish, the pieces radiating out from the centre like spokes in a wheel. Drizzle with melted butter. Bake at 400°F (200°C) for 20 minutes.

Serves 4

Pan-fried Bass

2 pounds (1kg)	bass fillets or 4 small bass
2 tsp (10mL)	salt
	freshly ground pepper
	juice of 1 lemon
½ cup (125mL)	flour
6 Tbsp (75mL)	butter
1 cup (250mL)	fresh bread crumbs
½ cup (125mL)	melted butter
¼ cup (50mL)	chopped parsley
4	lemon wedges, as garnish

Sprinkle fish with salt and pepper. Cover with lemon juice and set aside for 1 hour. Drain and dry well with paper towels. Dredge with flour.

Heat butter in a heavy frying pan. When foaming, add fish. When underside is slightly browned (2 to 3 minutes) turn fish over. Pile bread crumbs on top of each piece. Drizzle with melted butter. Transfer to a 400°F (200°C) oven and bake for 10 minutes.

To serve, sprinkle with chopped parsley and a little more melted butter. Garnish with lemon wedges.

Serves 4

Oxtail Stew

½ cup (125mL)	flour
½ tsp (2mL)	thyme
½ tsp (2mL)	salt
	freshly ground pepper
2 pounds (1kg)	oxtail cut in 2-inch (5-cm) lengths
2 Tbsp (25mL)	vegetable oil
2	bay leaves
2	garlic cloves, crushed
½ cup (125mL)	coarse barley
2 cups (500mL)	red wine
2 cups (500mL)	water (approx.)
4	small onions
1 dozen	cloves

Mix the flour, thyme, salt, and pepper together in a small plastic bag. Shake the oxtail pieces in the flour to coat evenly.

Heat oil in a heavy casserole. Add oxtail, turning frequently to brown evenly. Add bay leaves, garlic, barley, wine, and enough water to cover the meat. Stir together to mix well.

Cook, covered, at 350°F (180°C) for at least 4 hours. Halfway through cooking, add onions which have been stuck with cloves, and more water if stew has become too thick.

Serves 6

Molly Lamb Bobak, *Dinner in the Kitchen (No. 4),* 1943. Pencil on paper, 39.4 cm × 30.5 cm. Collection of the Art Gallery of Ontario.

Claude Breeze

Claude Breeze finds relaxation from painting and teaching at York University in Toronto through cooking, "particularly in chopping up the vegetables for Chinese dishes.

"We really enjoy Chinese meals, and often prepare them for ourselves and a couple of friends, but never for more than four people at a time.

"I remember a while back when we prepared a soup and two wok dishes every single night for two weeks straight. I also remember watching a television program once in which someone cooked spaghetti with olives. It looked terrific, so every night for a whole week I fooled around with the ingredients in different proportions until I got what I wanted."

Then there was the time he walked home from work daily past a pastry shop — and every night he dropped in for an assortment of sweets to take home for dessert. "It was madness. I solved it by taking a different route home. And since then, I've been avoiding desserts."

.... me wining + dining on a sunny summer's 1960 day by the sea

Wrapped Fish Fillets with Vegetables

4	large lettuce leaves
4	large mushrooms, finely chopped
2	green onions, finely chopped
¼ tsp (1mL)	fennel
½ tsp (2mL)	salt
	freshly ground pepper
4	large fillets of sole or cod
1½ cups (375mL)	dry white wine
3	stalks celery, sliced diagonally
4	carrots, sliced diagonally
4	green onions, sliced
¼ tsp (1mL)	oregano
¼ tsp (1mL)	thyme
	salt and pepper

Steam lettuce leaves for 2 minutes or until soft. Make a stuffing by combining mushrooms, green onion, fennel, salt, and pepper and divide evenly among fish. Fold fillets around stuffing. Wrap in lettuce leaves, securing with toothpicks.

Pour wine into a deep-sided frying pan. Add fillets and simmer, covered, for 5 minutes. Remove fish to a heated platter and keep warm.

Add remaining ingredients to the wine. Simmer, covered, for 5 minutes. Remove half the vegetables and reserve. Place fish on top of remaining vegetables in the frying pan, and cover with reserved vegetables. Add more wine, if necessary, to cover. Simmer for 10 minutes.

Serve with new potatoes.

Serves 4

Chicken Wings

10	chicken wings

Marinade

2 Tbsp (25mL)	soy sauce
2 Tbsp (25mL)	oyster sauce
1 Tbsp (15mL)	peanut oil
1 tsp (5mL)	brown sugar
1	garlic clove, crushed
1 Tbsp (15mL)	grated fresh ginger root

Place chicken wings in a single layer in a baking pan. Brush with marinade. Let sit for 1 hour. Bake at 375°F (190°C) for 40 minutes.

Serve on a bed of shredded lettuce.

Serves 2

Roast Rabbit for Two

1	small rabbit
1 tsp (5mL)	thyme
1 tsp (5mL)	oregano
1 tsp (5mL)	rosemary
1 tsp (5mL)	basil
2 Tbsp (25mL)	soft butter
¼ cup (50mL)	cognac

Rinse out cavity of rabbit and dry with paper towels. Combine herbs and rub them into cavity. Rub butter over outside of rabbit.

Place in a shallow roasting pan. Cook, uncovered, at 350°F (180°C) for 1½ hours, basting frequently. Remove to a warm platter. Flame with heated cognac.

Serves 2

Claude Breeze, . . . *me wining and dining on a sunny summer's 1980 day by the sea,* 1981. Pen and ink on paper, 36 cm × 28 cm. Collection of the artist. Photo: Mladen P. Kasalica.

Quick and Fresh for Two

lettuce for 2 people (use a variety and include some spinach)
6 large mushrooms, finely chopped
half a red pepper, diced
half a green pepper, diced
½ cup (125mL) water chestnuts, diced
1½ cups (375mL) sliced cooked chicken
4 green onions, cut in julienne strips
sesame seeds

Sauce
2 Tbsp (25mL) Hoisin sauce (available in Oriental specialty shops)
2 Tbsp (25mL) lemon juice
3 Tbsp (40mL) peanut oil
1 Tbsp (15mL) maple syrup
1 tsp (5mL) sesame oil

Cover bottom of a large platter with torn or shredded lettuce. Layer on the remaining ingredients. Just before serving, drizzle sauce over chicken and vegetables. Sprinkle with sesame seeds.

Serve on a bed of hot rice.

Serves 2

Pork in Marsala

Marinade
2 cups (500mL) Marsala
salt and pepper
½ tsp (2mL) ground coriander
½ tsp (2mL) garam masala (see page 193)
½ tsp (2mL) thyme
½ tsp (2mL) nutmeg
1 bay leaf
2 garlic cloves, crushed
2 green onions, chopped

4 pork tenderloins, each weighing approximately ¾ pound (375g)
4 Tbsp (50mL) butter
10 pearl onions, glazed in a little butter
½ pound (250g) green grapes

Combine marinade ingredients. Trim the fat and membrane from pork tenderloin and discard. Cut each tenderloin into 8 or 10 pieces. Cover with the marinade and set aside, covered, for 4 hours or overnight in the refrigerator. Turn meat occasionally.

Wipe meat dry. In a heavy frying pan, heat butter. Sauté meat until brown on all sides. Add marinade and more Marsala, if necessary, to cover. Simmer, covered, for 40 minutes. Add onions. Simmer for 15 minutes. Add grapes and simmer for 5 minutes.

Serve on a bed of rice.

Serves 4

Dennis Burton, *Maple Sugar,* 1967. Oil on masonite, 152.4 cm × 152.4 cm. Private collection.

Dennis Burton

"If you had a background like mine, you wouldn't be excited about gourmet food either," says Toronto painter Dennis Burton. "In the first place, my mother couldn't really cook. She always put mint in the vegetables and thought it was elegant. And during the war, I grew up on National Velvet. That's what we called it, but it was really horsemeat. There was a lot of bologna too, but no chocolate. After the war ended, though, I made up for my deprivation — I ate thousands of chocolate bars."

Things didn't much improve when, in the 1950s, teenaged Dennis was awarded a scholarship to attend a boys' school. "It was then that I really came to hate food. Every Friday for two years I ate 'Sewer Carp.' No wonder I got turned off. I used to be crazy about ice cream too — until I spent two summers working in a dairy. That cured me."

Fortunately Dennis met and married fellow painter Diane Pugen, and it's she who looks after the family's meals now, although most of her creative time in the kitchen is limited to weekends when she stocks the freezer for the forthcoming week.

"We're really exhausted from teaching at Art's Sake [the Toronto art school] by the time we get home at night," says Dennis, "so mostly we eat flopped in front of the television set. It's very relaxing, but you find when you go out to eat with friends that it's hard to sit properly at a table and talk. With TV eating, one loses one's manners."

Dennis has tried cooking. "Once upon a time, I bought a cookbook called *Men Cooking* or something like that. It was all about famous men in history who cooked. I used to make a lot of peanut butter sandwiches, but I got off them and onto lettuce and tomato instead. I do a mean ham and fried egg on brown toast with ketchup. And if I have to, I can make salads. I do my

best with these when it's very late and I'm very drunk, and I find myself very hungry.

"I used to cremate steak too — smothered with steak sauce, Escoffier sauce, any other kind of sauce I could find, garlic powder, anything — but I'd never remember to turn it over under the grill. It would be pretty much overcooked and charred so no one else would eat it.

"On second thought, I could probably be a gourmet if I worked at it."

Spaghetti Sauce

1 pound (500g)	ground beef
1	onion, diced
1	green pepper, diced
3	garlic cloves, crushed
½ pound (250g)	mushrooms, sliced
1 tsp (5mL)	salt
	freshly ground pepper
2 14-ounce (398-mL)	cans tomato sauce
1 tsp (5mL)	basil
1 tsp (5mL)	rosemary
1 tsp (5mL)	thyme
1 tsp (5mL)	oregano
1 tsp (5mL)	tarragon
½ tsp (2mL)	savory
½ tsp (2mL)	marjoram
¼ tsp (1mL)	anise
¼ tsp (1mL)	fennel
2 Tbsp (25mL)	brown sugar
2 Tbsp (25mL)	vinegar
1 pound (500g)	soy noodles
¼ cup (50mL)	chopped parsley

Sauté ground beef, diced onion, green pepper, garlic, and sliced mushrooms in a heavy frying pan until the meat is browned. Drain off any fat or liquid. Add salt and pepper to taste.

Combine tomato sauce, herbs, sugar, and vinegar in a medium saucepan. Simmer, covered, for 15 minutes. Add meat mixture and heat through.

Cook soy noodles in boiling salted water until *al dente* (tender yet firm) — about 8 to 10 minutes. Drain.

To serve, pour sauce over noodles and sprinkle with chopped parsley.

Serves 4

Spaghetti with Meatballs

1 pound (500g)	ground round steak
1	onion, diced
3	garlic cloves, crushed
1 tsp (5mL)	salt
	freshly ground pepper
½ cup (125mL)	wheat germ
1	egg
1 tsp (5mL)	thyme
1 tsp (5mL)	savory
¼ cup (50mL)	soy flour
	vegetable oil for frying
	Spaghetti Sauce, omitting ground beef and vegetables
1 pound (500g)	cooked soy noodles

Combine all ingredients except the soy flour, vegetable oil, Spaghetti Sauce and noodles.

Form into balls the size of a walnut. Dredge in flour and sauté in hot oil until cooked through, turning constantly to brown evenly — about 20 minutes.

When meatballs are cooked, add them to the spaghetti sauce. Serve spooned over cooked soy noodles.

Serves 4

Chicken Breasts with Pineapple Sauce

Pineapple Sauce
1 19-ounce (540-mL) can crushed pineapple, drained
1 onion, diced
1 garlic clove, crushed
1 14-ounce (398-mL) can tomato sauce
2 Tbsp (25mL) brown sugar
1 tsp (5mL) salt
freshly ground pepper
½ tsp (2mL) savory
½ tsp (2mL) thyme
¼ tsp (1mL) sage
3 Tbsp (40mL) soy sauce
2 Tbsp (25mL) vinegar

6 chicken breasts
½ cup (125mL) whole wheat flour
¼ cup (50mL) vegetable oil
1 green pepper, sliced
2 tomatoes, cut in quarters

Make pineapple sauce by combining all sauce ingredients in a saucepan and simmering, covered, over medium heat, for 10 minutes. Stir occasionally.

Wash and dry chicken breasts. Dredge in flour. Shake to remove excess. Heat oil in large casserole set over medium heat. Add chicken, skin side down and sauté until golden, turning once. If a quantity of fat accumulates, drain off until no more than ¼ cup (50mL) remains.

Pour pineapple sauce over chicken. Bake in a 350°F (180°C) oven for 45 minutes. Arrange green pepper slices and tomato quarters on top and bake for an additional 10 minutes.

Serves 6

Chicken Breasts with Tomato and Green Onions

Sauce
1 cup (250mL) tomato paste
1 cup (250mL) tomato juice
½ cup (125mL) chopped green onion
juice of 1 lemon
2 Tbsp (25mL) brown sugar
1 tsp (5mL) prepared mustard
1 tsp (5mL) dry mustard
1 tsp (5mL) tarragon
2 garlic cloves, crushed
salt and freshly ground pepper
dash of cayenne

6 chicken breasts
½ cup (125mL) whole wheat flour
¼ cup (50mL) vegetable oil

To make sauce, combine ingredients and set aside. Wash and dry chicken breasts. Dredge in flour. Shake to remove excess. Heat oil in a large casserole. Add chicken, skin side down, and sauté until golden, turning once. Drain off excess fat so no more than ¼ cup (50mL) remains.

Pour sauce over chicken. Bake at 350°F (180°C) for 1 hour, basting chicken pieces occasionally.

Serves 6

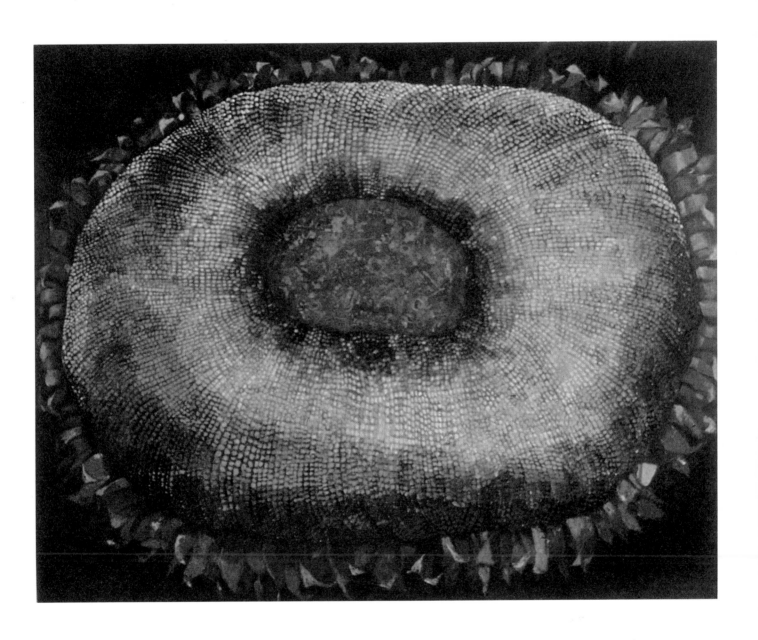

Ghitta Caiserman-Roth, *Sunflower No. 5,* 1965. Oil on
board, 127 cm × 157 cm. CIL Art Collection.

Ghitta Caiserman-Roth

Whenever Ghitta Caiserman-Roth is interested in something, it is with whole-hearted enthusiasm. It may be painting, teaching, travelling, tennis — or food.

"Max and I are in a gourmet group that gets together once a month in different homes. I've been taking lessons in Chinese cooking, so I'm getting ready to serve the group a Chinese meal the next time it's our turn. It will be a refreshing change from French cuisine."

Ghitta and her architect husband Max Roth both enjoy good food and cooking together in their Westmount home. They are also very concerned about nutrition, using egg substitutes where possible to cut down on cholesterol intake, and making sure that the refrigerator is always well stocked with a bowl of *crudités* for nibbling and between-meal snacks. Ghitta is a "good cook with vegetables" and is known among friends as an eggplant specialist.

"It's Max, though, who is the real gourmet cook," Ghitta says. "He has a special way with fish. When we entertain, I work around him. I do things at either end of the meal — I'm the beginning and ending person. He'll likely do a major fish production, maybe a garnished sea bass surrounded by a garden of tomatoes and greenery. I may do a soup or a *crêpe* dish for the first course, and the dessert.

"We're very visually oriented about food. We bought some black plates in Mexico which gave inspiration to our creation, Poires noires. They are a sort of variation on Poires Hélène. One night when we were planning to serve that for dessert, we had four extra, unexpected guests turn up and no more pears so we had to figure out quickly how to expand dessert. We cut apples into wedges and dipped them in melted chocolate and out came another new creation! It was one of our more successful ventures."

On a normal day, Max and Ghitta will have a quiet dinner together late at night. Then on weekends they head for their cottage, which they share with another couple. "The best part of it," says Ghitta, "are the breakfasts the men take turns making for us!"

Ghitta's Eggplant Dip

1	medium eggplant
	juice of half a lemon
1 Tbsp (15mL)	olive oil
½ tsp (2mL)	salt
	freshly ground pepper
¼ cup (50mL)	chopped parsley
1	medium sour pickle, finely chopped
1	medium onion, finely chopped
¼ cup (50mL)	mayonnaise
	bread crumbs (optional)

Wash eggplant and with a sharp knife, pierce the skin in several places. Put on a baking pan and bake at 350°F (180°C) for about 30 minutes or until soft.

Peel eggplant, discarding skin, and put pulp in a blender. Add lemon juice, olive oil, salt, pepper and parsley. Blend briefly to combine. Stir in the chopped pickle, onion and mayonnaise. If the dip requires thickening, gradually add small amounts of fine bread crumbs.

Pour into a small serving bowl and use as a dip for black bread or *crudités* (raw vegetables), or serve as a first course on crisp lettuce leaves.

Yield: 2 cups (500mL)

Cold Soup Easy

1 10-ounce (300-g)	package frozen vegetables (e.g. green beans or spinach or cauliflower or peas)
1 tsp (5mL)	curry powder
¼ tsp (1mL)	salt
	freshly ground pepper
1 cup (250mL)	natural yoghurt
2	black olives, sliced
2	lemon wedges

Cook a package of frozen vegetables as directed. When cooked, put the vegetables and cooking liquid in the container of a blender. Add curry powder, salt, and pepper. Purée until smooth. Add yoghurt and blend briefly. Chill well.

Serve cold, garnished with olive slices and a lemon wedge.

Serves 2

Chocolate Apples

4 ounces (100g)	unsweetened chocolate
2 ounces (50g)	semi-sweet chocolate
2 Tbsp (25mL)	unsalted butter
2 Tbsp (25mL)	white crème de menthe
6	firm apples
2 cups (500mL)	finely chopped walnuts

Melt both kinds of chocolate and the butter in a small bowl set in a pan of hot, but not boiling, water. Stir in crème de menthe.

Peel apples, remove cores, and cut each into 8 wedges. Using 2 toothpicks or small forks, dip each wedge into melted chocolate and then roll in chopped nuts.

Chill on a baking pan lined with waxed paper. When chocolate is set transfer apple wedges to a cookie tin and store covered, in the refrigerator. They will keep for up to 36 hours without "weeping."

Serves 8

Poires noires

1 cup (250mL)	granulated sugar
4 cups (1L)	water
	juice of 1 lemon
2	cinnamon sticks
4	cloves
1 Tbsp (15mL)	grenadine
6	firm pears, stems intact
4 ounces (100g)	unsweetened chocolate
2 ounces (50g)	semi-sweet chocolate
2 Tbsp (25mL)	unsalted butter
	fresh mint leaves, or crystallized mint leaves, or crystallized flowers for garnish

Dissolve sugar in water. Add lemon juice, cinnamon sticks, cloves, and grenadine. Simmer for 15 minutes. Peel pears, leaving stems intact, and cut a slice off the bottom of each so it will stand upright.

Poach pears in simmering syrup, covered, until tender (25 to 40 minutes depending on the type of pears). Cool in the syrup, then chill.

Melt both kinds of chocolate and the butter in a small bowl set in a pan of hot, not boiling, water.

Remove pears from syrup and dry well with paper towels. Dip each pear in chocolate using a spoon to coat evenly.

Chill on a baking pan lined with waxed paper.

To serve, place each pear on an individual plate and decorate with mint leaves or crystallized flowers. Pears will keep up to 36 hours in the refrigerator without "weeping."

Serves 6

Crème de menthe Cookies

¾ cup (175mL)	butter
¾ cup (175mL)	sugar
½ tsp (2mL)	salt
2	egg yolks
1 Tbsp (15mL)	cream
1 tsp (5mL)	vanilla
2 cups (500mL)	flour

Chocolate Glaze

4 ounces (100g)	semi-sweet chocolate
2 Tbsp (25mL)	butter
1 Tbsp (15mL)	white crème de menthe
	finely chopped walnuts

Cream butter until light and fluffy. Gradually add sugar and continue beating. Add salt, egg yolks, cream, and vanilla. Slowly add flour to form a stiff dough.

Divide dough in half, press into a flat square shape, and wrap each half in waxed paper. Chill for 2 hours. Roll out to ¼-inch (5-mm) thickness. Cut into finger sticks. Arrange sticks on a lightly greased baking pan. Bake at 325°F (160°C) for 15 minutes or until golden. Remove to a wire rack to cool.

To make glaze, combine chocolate, butter and crème de menthe in a bowl set over hot water. Stir until mixture is melted.

Dip end of each cookie in chocolate glaze and then in chopped walnuts.

Yield: 5 dozen

Ian Carr-Harris

"How you serve a meal is, of course, your affair. It involves a total summation of what you are — barring to some degree the odd inappropriate interjection of Fate."

That is a typical Ian Carr-Harris comment. The Toronto sculptor approaches food in much the same careful conceptual manner as he does his constructions, and he sees food and art as very similar creative acts and expressions.

"I used to cook a lot more than I do now, but I still like to have six or eight friends for dinner. We all gather around the table and a whole social situation is set up. It's a very aesthetic performance."

Ian plans with care the meals he serves to guests. "I balance the items on the menu from the point of view of the palate. I think it's very unwise to serve a lot of heavy things, or foods that are similar in texture or in any other way.

"When selecting the foods I serve to friends," he says, "a sense of visual aesthetics prevails. These visuals are quite intuitive to an artist, I think. At least they are to me."

Ian has good advice for starting the day right. "Scones and cornbread served with coffee and hot milk, and perhaps a few strips of bacon if you are hungry or have company, make a very easy and pleasant introduction to the day. A breakfast like this will enable you to suffer the inevitable fools you will run into or otherwise encounter in the next twenty-four hours with greater aplomb and enhanced efficiency."

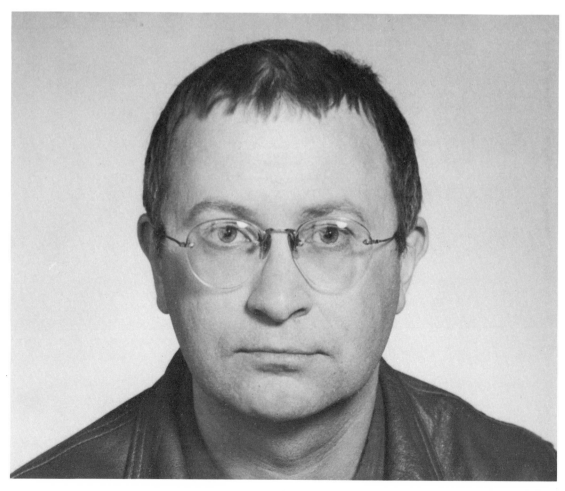

Honey Bread

¼ cup (50mL)	lukewarm water
1 Tbsp (15mL)	sugar
1 package	yeast
1	egg
½ cup (125mL)	honey
1 Tbsp (15mL)	ground coriander
½ tsp (2mL)	ground cinnamon
¼ tsp (1mL)	ground cloves
1 tsp (5mL)	salt
1 cup (250mL)	lukewarm milk
4 Tbsp (50mL)	unsalted butter, melted
3½ to 4 cups (850mL to 1L)	all-purpose flour (approx.)

In a small bowl, dissolve sugar in water. Sprinkle in yeast. Set aside for 10 minutes.

In a large bowl, beat egg with a wire whisk. Stir in honey, coriander, cinnamon, cloves, and salt. Add the yeast mixture, lukewarm milk, and melted butter. Add flour, a cup at a time, beating well with a spoon. When mixture becomes too thick and heavy to continue beating, turn out onto a floured board and knead in enough remaining flour to form a stiff dough.

Knead until dough is smooth and elastic — 5 to 10 minutes.

Shape dough into a ball and place in a large buttered bowl, turning dough so all sides are buttered. Cover with a towel and set to rise in a warm, draft-free place until double in bulk — about 1½ hours.

Butter well a 2-quart (2-L) soufflé dish or casserole. Punch dough down and knead on floured board for 2 to 3 minutes. Shape into a ball and place in prepared dish, pressing dough out to the edges at the bottom. Cover with a towel and set to rise in a warm place for 1 to 2 hours, until it has risen 1 inch (2.5cm) above the top rim of the dish.

Bake at 350°F (180°C) for 1 hour. Remove from dish and cool on a wire rack.

Scones

2 cups (475mL)	flour
4 tsp (20mL)	baking powder
½ tsp (2mL)	salt
½ cup (125mL)	firm butter
1	egg
⅓ cup (75mL)	milk (approx.)

Sift together flour, baking powder, and salt. Cut in butter with a pastry blender or 2 knives until mixture resembles coarse meal.

Beat egg with a fork in a 1-cup (250-mL) measure. Add enough milk to reach ¾-cup (175-mL) mark. Quickly stir the liquid into the dry ingredients, using hands if necessary, to get a slightly dry, springy dough.

Pat dough into a circle 1 inch (2.5cm) thick on a greased baking pan. Cut into 2-inch (5-cm) squares or triangles and separate pieces slightly.

Bake at 425°F (220°C) for 10 to 15 minutes or until lightly golden. Serve warm.

Yield: 1 dozen

Cornbread

1 cup (250mL)	flour
¾ cup (175mL)	cornmeal
½ cup (125mL)	brown sugar
3 tsp (15mL)	baking powder
¾ tsp (5mL)	salt
1	egg
1 cup (250mL)	milk

Combine dry ingredients in a large bowl. Beat egg well then add milk. Stir into dry ingredients. Batter should be runny but not liquid. Add a little more milk if necessary.

Pour into greased 8-inch (2-L) square pan. Bake at 425°F (220°C) for 25 minutes. Cut into squares and serve warm.

Yield: 16 squares

Crème flamande
Cream of Potato Soup

4	large onions
3	medium potatoes, diced
1 tsp (5mL)	salt
	water
2 Tbsp (25mL)	butter
¼ cup (50mL)	chopped parsley
½ cup (125mL)	table cream

Coarsely chop 3 of the onions and place them with the diced potatoes and salt in a medium saucepan. Add enough water to cover. Bring to the boil, reduce heat, and simmer, covered, until soft — about 15 minutes.

Purée the vegetables and liquid in a blender or food processor until smooth. Return to saucepan.

Slice the remaining onion very thin. Sauté slices in butter until soft and golden — do not allow to brown. Add to soup for 5 minutes.

Stir in parsley and cream and heat through but do not allow to boil.

Serves 4

Nun's Chicken Pie

Chicken Mixture

4 pounds (2kg)	chicken
1 cup (250mL)	celery leaves
3	medium onions, cut in quarters
4	bay leaves
1 Tbsp (15mL)	salt
½ tsp (2mL)	pepper
1 tsp (5mL)	thyme
6 cups (1.5L)	water

Place all ingredients in a large saucepan and simmer, covered, for 1 hour or until chicken is tender. Remove chicken and set aside. Boil liquid, uncovered, until it is reduced to 2 cups (500mL), then strain.

Remove chicken meat and skin from bones, leaving meat in large chunks. Discard the bones. Place skin in a blender and add ¼ cup (50mL) reduced chicken stock. Purée until creamy. Pour into a 2-cup (500-mL) measure and add enough stock to reach 1¾-cup (400-mL) mark. Set aside. Reserve remaining stock.

Vegetable Mixture

3 cups (750mL)	thinly sliced carrots
2 cups (500mL)	thinly sliced celery
1 dozen	pearl onions
½ cup (125mL)	chopped parsley
¾ cup (175mL)	butter
1 cup (250mL)	flour
1 cup (250mL)	milk
1 Tbsp (15mL)	lemon juice

Steam carrots, celery, onions, and parsley until just tender — about 8 to 10 minutes. Drain and set aside.

In medium saucepan, melt butter. Add flour and cook for 1 minute, stirring constantly. Slowly add milk and reserved puréed skin mixture. Cook, stirring until smooth and thickened.

Add the vegetable mixture and lemon juice. Carefully mix in chicken pieces and set aside.

Pastry

3 cups (750mL)	flour
3 tsp (15mL)	baking powder
1 tsp (5mL)	salt
½ pound (250g)	lard
⅓ cup (75mL)	reserved chicken broth or water (approx.)

To make the pastry, sift together the flour, baking powder, and salt. Cut in the lard using a pastry blender or 2 knives until mixture resembles coarse meal. Stir in the broth and, using hands, form into 2 balls, one slightly larger than the other. Wrap separately in waxed paper and chill for 1 hour.

Roll out larger ball of pastry and use it to line a 2½-quart (2-L) round, deep baking dish or casserole. Pour in chicken mixture. Roll out smaller ball of pastry, fit it over top of filling and trim. Moisten the edges to seal and crimp together with the tines of a fork.

With a sharp knife, cut 6 vent holes in top crust to allow steam to escape.

Bake at 400°F (200°C) for 30 to 35 minutes or until golden brown.

Serves 6

Couscous Tagine

Conserie d'harissa

2 Tbsp (25mL)	cayenne
1 Tbsp (15mL)	cumin
2	garlic cloves, crushed
½ tsp (2mL)	salt
1 cup (250mL)	olive oil

Meat and Vegetable Mixture

¼ cup (50mL)	olive oil (more as needed)
2 pounds (1kg)	lamb, cut in 1-inch (2.5-cm) pieces
4 pounds (2kg)	chicken, cut in pieces
4	carrots, cut in 2-inch (5-cm) sticks
2	medium onions, cut in chunks
3	celery stalks, cut in 2-inch (5-cm) pieces
3	cinnamon sticks
10	peppercorns, lightly crushed
10	whole cloves
1 tsp (5mL)	cumin
¼ tsp (1mL)	saffron
2 tsp (10mL)	salt
½ tsp (2mL)	pepper
4	tomatoes, peeled, seeded and cut in chunks
8 cups (2L)	chicken stock to cover (approx.)
2 cups (500mL)	cooked chick peas
2	sweet potatoes, peeled and cut in slices
2	small turnips, peeled and cut in small chunks
1 pound (500g)	zucchini, cut in small chunks
1 pound (500g)	artichoke hearts, cut in quarters

Couscous

3 cups (750mL)	couscous grains
	water
4 Tbsp (50mL)	olive oil
6 Tbsp (75mL)	melted butter
2 tsp (10mL)	salt

Garnishes

lemon wedges
parsley clusters

To make the *conserie d'harissa*, grind ingredients together in a blender. Pour into a small saucepan and cook over medium heat for 5 minutes. Stir before using, as the solid ingredients settle to the bottom.

To make meat and vegetable mixture, heat olive oil in a large frying pan. Sauté lamb, chicken, carrots, and onion chunks, a few pieces at time, so as not to overcrowd. Drain off moisture that may accumulate and add more olive oil as necessary. When well browned, transfer pieces to a large stewing pot or *couscousière*.

Into the *couscousière* put the celery pieces, cinnamon sticks, peppercorns, cloves, cumin, 2 teaspoons (10mL) *conserie d'harissa*, saffron, salt, pepper, tomato chunks, and chicken stock. Cover and simmer for 10 minutes.

Add the chick peas, sweet potato slices, and turnip chunks. Cook, covered, for 20 minutes.

To prepare the couscous grains, soak them in cold water to cover for 5 minutes, fluffing once with the fingers or 2 forks.

Line a steamer or the top of the *couscousière* with a double layer of cheesecloth. Drain the couscous and steam it over boiling water or over the meat mixture in the *couscousière* for 15 minutes. Turn it out onto a warm platter and sprinkle with the 4 tablespoons (50mL) olive oil, while rolling the grains between the fingers. Set aside in a warm place.

Add the zucchini chunks and artichoke hearts to the meat mixture. Simmer for 15 minutes, then return the couscous to the cheesecloth-lined steamer. Cover and steam for 10 minutes.

To serve, toss the couscous with butter and salt. Place a mound of the couscous in a circle around the edges of a large, round, heated platter. Pour the meat and vegetable mixture into the well in the centre, removing the cinnamon sticks.

Garnish with lemon wedges and parsley clusters. Sprinkle hot *conserie d'harissa* over the couscous and serve.

Serves 10

A.J. Casson

When he is at home in Toronto, A.J. Casson is well fed and taken care of by his wife. "However, if she is tied up or busy," he says, "I'll do the cooking, but it will be something plain. I can cook all the plain things."

Over the years, his cooking expertise has been developed on sketching trips in northern Ontario, many of them in the company of the other members of the Group of Seven. "When you're out in the country and woods, you're carrying so much painting equipment that you don't have much room for cooking utensils, so anything you do has to be simple. And then, too, you want to have every minute possible for painting, so you don't want to take the time for cooking. Up on the Magnetewan River we used to cook a lot of fish, especially Magnetewan bass.

"When Joe Gauthier and I went on sketching trips in the late fall, we always wanted a bowl of hot soup when we came in from a long cold day. We soon got tired of canned and dry soups.

"Then I remembered something my grandmother used to make when I was a small boy. It was a hearty soup made in the frying pan from onions and tomatoes cooked in the fat left over from our morning bacon. That became our starter night after night and it worked every time."

Sketching-Trip Soup

2 Tbsp (25mL)	bacon fat
1	large Spanish onion, sliced
6	large ripe tomatoes, cut in wedges
	salt and pepper

Heat the fat in a heavy frying pan. Sauté onion slices until limp. Stir in tomato wedges. Add salt and pepper. Cover pan and simmer over low heat for 30 minutes or until vegetables are very soft and form a thick soup.

Serves 2

Alan Collier

As Alan Collier sits in the comfortable living room of his Toronto home, the winter sun streams in through large windows, giving a sparkle to the elegant furnishings and *objets d'art* that combine to make the room so graceful. The adjoining dining room looks very inviting and welcoming — the setting for many an enjoyable evening.

When Alan and Ruth Collier, who like to entertain friends at dinner, talk about some of the foods they have served, tantalizing names like Mushroom Croustades and Banana Vichyssoise waft through the air.

"It's really Ruth who is in charge of the meals around here," says Alan. "She's the one responsible for our elegant dinners and for the everyday task of seeing that we're fed. I was brought up on basic things like Spanish Rice, and Ruth still makes my mother's recipe for it. I guess we have a lot of other 'hurry-up meals' too, particularly when I'm painting.

"I can take care of myself, don't get me wrong, and I do when I'm off on a sketching trip."

This is another side of Alan Collier. He spends several months of the year painting the Canadian landscapes for which he is so well known, far removed from the comforts of his Toronto home. He may be close by in northern Ontario, or he may be at the other end of the country. And he may be gone for months at a time, in which case Ruth will join him in their trailer.

"Obviously we eat in a very different style when we're away, but still, we eat well."

Ruth prepares the main meals in the trailer, packing sandwiches and snacks for Alan to take in his knapsack to be eaten throughout the day. Being hypoglycemic, Alan must nibble frequent high-protein snacks and Ruth has developed a substantial repertoire of varied and interesting recipes.

"I'm more inclined to do easy things when we're away," says Ruth, "so the Spanish Rice appears regularly, as do the Foiled Lamb Chops. They're good because they don't make any mess!"

Mushroom Croustades

12	thin slices white sandwich bread
4 Tbsp (50mL)	soft butter
3	green onions, coarsely chopped
2 Tbsp (25mL)	flour
½ tsp (2mL)	salt
dash of	cayenne
1 Tbsp (15mL)	parsley
1 tsp (5mL)	lemon juice
1 cup (250mL)	table cream, heated
½ pound (250g)	mushrooms, finely chopped
2 Tbsp (25mL)	grated Parmesan cheese
	parsley sprigs, as garnish

Trim crusts from bread. Roll flat with a rolling pin. Grease the insides of 12 large muffin tins using 2 tablespoons (25mL) of the butter. Firmly press a slice of bread into each cup. Bake at 400°F (200°C) for 10 minutes. Remove bread from cups and cool on a wire rack.

Put remaining 2 tablespoons (25mL) butter in a blender or food processor and add onions, flour, salt, cayenne, parsley, and lemon juice. Add hot cream. Blend briefly at high speed. Pour into saucepan and add chopped mushrooms. Cook over medium heat stirring constantly for 5 to 7 minutes or until thickened. Cool.

Just before serving, fill each croustade generously with the mushroom mixture. Sprinkle with Parmesan cheese. Bake at 350°F (180°C) for 20 minutes.

Serve hot, garnished with a parsley sprig.

Serves 6 as an appetizer

Banana Vichyssoise

1½ cups (375mL)	diced potatoes
1½ cups (375mL)	diced peeled apples
½ cup (125mL)	diced celery
2	bananas, sliced
4 cups (1L)	chicken stock
½ tsp (2mL)	salt
2 Tbsp (25mL)	melted butter
½ tsp (2mL)	curry powder
1 cup (250mL)	milk
1 cup (250mL)	skim milk powder
	grated lemon peel, as garnish

Bring to a boil the diced potatoes, apples, celery, bananas, chicken stock, and salt. Cover and simmer until potatoes are tender — about 15 minutes. Uncover and set aside to cool, then purée in a blender or food processor. Add butter, curry powder, milk, and milk powder and blend again for 30 seconds. Refrigerate, covered, for at least 6 hours.

To serve, sprinkle with grated lemon peel.

Serves 8

Spinach Salad

1 10-ounce (284-g)	package fresh spinach
1 10-ounce (284-mL)	can water chestnuts, drained and sliced thin
	salt and pepper
2 Tbsp (25mL)	toasted sesame seeds

	Dressing
3 Tbsp (40mL)	water
2 Tbsp (25mL)	cider vinegar
2 Tbsp (25mL)	soy sauce
4 tsp (20mL)	vegetable oil
½ tsp (2mL)	sugar
¼ tsp (1mL)	powdered ginger
1	garlic clove, crushed

Wash and dry spinach well, discarding tough stems. Toss with sliced water chestnuts, salt and pepper.

Combine all dressing ingredients. Pour over spinach and toss to coat evenly. Sprinkle with sesame seeds.

Serves 6

Spanish Rice

½ pound (250g)	ground beef
¼ cup (50mL)	diced onion
¼ cup (50mL)	diced green pepper
1 28-ounce (796-mL)	can tomatoes
1 tsp (5mL)	salt
¼ tsp (1mL)	pepper
1 tsp (5mL)	sugar
2 tsp (10mL)	Worcestershire sauce
¾ cup (175mL)	Minute Rice

Sauté the beef, onion, and green pepper in a heavy saucepan. Add the tomatoes with their liquid, salt, pepper, sugar, and Worcestershire sauce. Bring to a boil, stirring to break up the tomatoes.

Add rice. Cover and turn off heat. Let stand for 10 minutes.

Serves 2 generously

Foiled Lamb Chops

8	shoulder lamb chops
4	small potatoes, peeled and quartered
8	carrots, halved crosswise
4	medium onions, quartered
4	chunks green pepper
	salt and pepper

Cut 4 strips of heavy foil each 18 inches (45cm) in length. Put 2 lamb chops in the middle of each piece. Top each pair of lamb chops with 4 potato quarters, 4 carrot halves, 4 onion chunks, and a piece of green pepper. Sprinkle with salt and pepper.

Wrap each piece of foil securely. Place on a baking pan and bake at 325°F (160°C) for 2 hours or at 275°F (140°C) for 3 hours.

Serves 4

Protein Snack

½ cup (125mL)	peanut butter
4 Tbsp (50mL)	skim milk powder
½ cup (125mL)	raisins
4 Tbsp (50mL)	toasted sesame seeds

Mix peanut butter, powdered milk, and raisins together. Roll into a log about 1½ inches (4cm) in diameter.

Cut into 10 pieces and roll each in toasted sesame seeds. Store in refrigerator.

Good trail food or for a mid-morning or afternoon pick-me-up.

Yield: 10 pieces

Alex Colville

Alex Colville loves salads. A well-tended vegetable garden in the backyard of his Wolfville home may have something to do with it, although he says he'll devour salads any time of the year, and at any meal — before the main course, after the main course, or as the main course.

"It's a big debate, isn't it, when one 'ought to' serve the salad? I'll eat salads any time, but if I had to make a choice, I guess I'd choose to have mine before the entrée."

Alex Colville is an inventive cook. "Last week, I was rummaging around in the fridge, and I found some pound cake. So I sliced it up, spiked it with some sherry, smothered it with whipped cream, cut up some bananas and strawberries, and had the most marvellous dessert. I don't worry about calories and cholesterol. I love food so I eat — eggs, butter, cream. They don't seem to bother me and I'm healthy."

The Colvilles obviously enjoy food. "One cooks to a common denominator when you have four children and they all like different things," he says, "but now that they're all grown and living away from home, our meals are much more interesting. We also drink wine with our dinners, a habit we picked up while living in California in the late sixties."

The children, he says, are all great cooks themselves, probably from having been exposed to good food when they were at home. Still, it's Rhoda Colville on whom the family's greatest praise is lavished for being the real chef. She has always baked their bread, and, according to Alex, makes the world's best strawberry shortcake.

Dinner guests at the Colville home may be treated to Rhoda's famous seafood casserole, or Sole Florentine. But of all the things she makes, her husband's favourite is a meat pie from a recipe that has been in the family for generations.

"I like to have some good beef gravy on hand for thickening the meat mixture," says Rhoda, "but mushroom soup seems foolproof and good too." Accompanied by a salad, it's the perfect family meal.

Sole Florentine

1 pound (500g)	fresh spinach
½ tsp (2mL)	sugar
1 Tbsp (15mL)	butter
2 Tbsp (25mL)	flour
	freshly grated nutmeg
2 Tbsp (25mL)	table cream
6	small sole fillets
	salt and pepper
2 Tbsp (25mL)	butter
½ cup (125mL)	sliced mushrooms

Sauce

2 Tbsp (25mL)	butter
4 Tbsp (50mL)	flour
½ cup (125mL)	table cream
½ cup (125mL)	milk
½ cup (125mL)	grated Parmesan cheese
2 Tbsp (25mL)	chopped parsley

Wash spinach, discarding tough stems. Sprinkle with sugar. Place in a large saucepan and cook with the water that clings to the leaves. Stir frequently. Remove from heat when spinach is wilted. Do not drain. Add 1 tablespoon (15mL) butter, 2 tablespoons (25mL) flour, grated nutmeg, and 2 tablespoons (25mL) cream. Combine well.

Spread spinach evenly over bottom of a well-greased 9-inch (2.5-L) square pan. Cover with a layer of sole fillets. Sprinkle with salt and pepper.

Heat 2 tablespoons (25mL) butter in a small frying pan. Sauté the mushrooms until golden. Spread evenly over sole.

Make a white sauce by melting 2 tablespoons (25mL) butter and adding the 4 tablespoons (50mL) flour, ½ cup (125mL) cream, and milk. Stir over medium heat until smooth and thickened. Add Parmesan cheese and chopped parsley. Spoon over the fish. Bake at 375°F (190°C) for 30 minutes.

Serves 4

Fish Chowder

¼ pound (125g)   bacon
1   large onion, finely chopped
1   bunch celery, cut in ½-inch (1-cm) slices
6   medium potatoes, peeled and diced
2 pounds (1kg)   haddock fillets
   salt and pepper
1 cup (250mL)   water
4 cups (1L)   milk
2 Tbsp (25mL)   butter
   chopped parsley, as garnish

Cut bacon into small pieces and fry in a heavy saucepan. Remove with a slotted spoon. Add chopped onion to bacon fat and sauté until golden. Add celery and diced potatoes. Sprinkle fish on both sides with salt and pepper. Place fish on top of vegetables. Return bacon to saucepan. Pour in water, cover, and cook slowly until potatoes are done — about 45 minutes. Stir together to blend ingredients. Add milk and butter and heat through. Do not allow to boil.

Serve in heated bowls, topped with a sprinkling of parsley.

Serves 10 to 12

Succotash

10   large ears of corn
1 cup (250mL)   shelled beans (Kentucky Wonders, Jacob's Cattle, or lima, soaked overnight in water)
½ cup (125mL)   milk
2 Tbsp (25mL)   butter
1 tsp (5mL)   salt
   freshly ground pepper

Cut kernels from the ears of corn. Barely cover beans and corn with water and simmer until the beans are soft and mealy. Drain and add milk, butter, salt, and pepper. Heat through and serve immediately.

Serves 4

Meat Pie

Pastry
2¼ cups (550mL)   flour
1 tsp (5mL)   salt
1 Tbsp (15mL)   sugar
1 cup (250mL)   shortening
1   egg
   water

Filling
2 pounds (1kg)   ground round steak
1 tsp (5mL)   salt
   freshly ground pepper
1   garlic clove, crushed
1 tsp (5mL)   thyme
½ tsp (2mL)   celery salt
1 10-ounce (284-mL)   can cream of mushroom soup or 1 cup (250mL) thick gravy

To make the pastry, mix flour, salt, and sugar together in a bowl. Cut in shortening with a pastry blender or 2 knives until mixture resembles coarse meal. Break the egg into a 1-cup (250-mL) measure. Fill to the ½-cup (125-mL) mark with water. Mix together with a fork and combine with dry ingredients. Form into 2 balls. Wrap in waxed paper and chill for 30 minutes.

To make the filling, brown the meat in a heavy frying pan and add seasonings. Add mushroom soup or gravy. Set aside to cool. (If meat has released a lot of fat, pour it off before adding soup.)

Roll out a ball of pastry and use it to line a 9-inch (1-L) pie plate. Fill with meat. Roll out second ball and cover pie. Moisten edges and crimp together to seal. Brush top with cream or milk. Cut a few slits in the top with a sharp knife to allow steam to escape.

Bake at 400°F (200°C) for approximately 40 minutes or until pastry is golden brown.

Serves 4

Bread

1 tsp (5mL)	sugar
1 cup (250mL)	lukewarm water
2 packages	yeast
3 cups (750mL)	lukewarm water
2 Tbsp (25mL)	salt
6 Tbsp (75mL)	sugar
3 Tbsp (40mL)	shortening
10 cups (2.5L)	flour (all white, or a combination of white and whole wheat flours)

Dissolve sugar in 1 cup (250mL) lukewarm water in a small bowl. Add yeast and set aside for 10 minutes.

Pour 3 cups (750mL) warm water into a large bowl. Add the yeast mixture, salt, sugar, and shortening. Stir together well. Gradually add flour, turning out onto a floured board when dough becomes too thick to stir. Knead until smooth and elastic — for about 10 minutes. Return to a greased bowl, cover with a clean towel, and let rise in a warm place until double in bulk — about 1 hour.

Turn out of bowl and knead again. Shape into 4 loaves and place in greased loaf pans. Cover with a towel and let rise again — about 1 hour.

Bake at 400°F (200°C) for 5 minutes. Reduce heat to 350°F (180°C) and bake for a further 45 minutes.

Yield: 4 loaves

Strawberry Shortcake

2 cups (475mL)	sifted flour
4 tsp (20mL)	baking powder
½ tsp (2mL)	salt
⅓ cup (75mL)	sugar
½ cup (125mL)	shortening
½ cup (125mL)	whipping cream
¼ cup (50mL)	water
	butter
1 quart (1L)	strawberries, lightly crushed
1 cup (250mL)	whipping cream

Sift dry ingredients together. With a pastry blender or two knives, cut in shortening until mixture resembles coarse meal. Combine ½ cup (125mL) whipping cream and water. Quickly stir into dry ingredients until well mixed and a soft dough forms.

Spread half the dough in a 10-inch (25-cm) circle on a lightly greased baking pan. Flatten smoothly. Put remaining dough on top and spread out evenly.

Bake at 425°F (220°C) for 15 to 20 minutes. Split and butter while hot. Fill with crushed strawberries. Whip cream. Cover cake with whipped cream and more berries.

Serves 8

Graham Coughtry

"Look, you've got to love food if you're going to live above Switzer's," says painter Graham Coughtry of his Toronto home. "If I'm in a hurry, I'll run into the deli to grab a pastrami sandwich, but I always take it upstairs to my apartment. I rarely eat it in the restaurant."

Graham, who grew up in St. Lambert, Quebec, moved to Toronto as a teenager and later spent several years in Spain. "I love Spanish cuisine. When we lived there, we had our own orange grove.

"When I was much younger, I used to go fishing and hunting. It was a very macho thing to do, I now realize, and I can't believe that I ever did it — killed moose and deer, shot pheasant and grouse, and skinned rabbits. I just can't believe I did it, but I did make a great rabbit stew.

"I used to do a lot more gourmet cooking than I do now. I wooed my wife on things like *escargots* and *boeuf bourguignonne.* But now, I'm more inclined to throw together a huge pot of pea soup like my mother used to make — you know, with ham and lentils and split peas. I like it because once you've made it, it lasts forever.

"My recipe for the Guinea Fowl is as much a reminiscence as it is a recipe. It was concocted at a time — in the late fifties — when I was courting my wife and it seems magically, in retrospect, to contain the ingredients that prophesied our subsequent marriage and expatriate life on the Island of Ibiza off the southern coast of Spain. That is to say, it served its very romantic purpose, so, perhaps, beware.

"You should eat it with a bottle of chilled Meursault and follow with Spanish coffee or polish off the calvados. I would suggest music such as Debussy preludes played by Aldo Ciccolini, any good flamenco guitar, Coltrane ballads, or Nights in the Garden of Spain by de Falla performed by Gonzalo Soriano. If all this sounds like an attempt at seduction — it is.

"As for the Distant Island Soup, it is especially suited to those bleak days when I have the feeling that far away islands look greener and usually are. The recipe can be modified to fit anyone's real or imagined escape."

Distant Island Soup

3	cans "Bon Vivant" green turtle consommé
1 cup (250mL)	Portuguese *vinho verde* (white wine)
1 cup (250mL)	split green peas
½ cup (125mL)	fresh or frozen green peas
1 Tbsp (15mL)	lime juice
½ cup (125mL)	chopped green onions
½ cup (125mL)	chopped celery
½ cup (125mL)	diced green pepper
½ cup (125mL)	chopped mushrooms
1	garlic clove, crushed
1 Tbsp (15mL)	olive oil
1	bay leaf
2	coriander leaves
1 tsp (5mL)	basil
1 tsp (5mL)	dill
6	green peppercorns, crushed
pinch each of	marjoram, rosemary, and thyme
½ cup (125mL)	commercial sour cream
1 Tbsp (15mL)	Roquefort cheese
1 cup (250mL)	chopped green onion stalks
1 cup (250mL)	diced green pepper
1 cup (250mL)	chopped celery
½ cup (125mL)	green peas
1 Tbsp (15mL)	marijuana (in jurisdictions where legal)
¼ cup (50mL)	pale dry sherry

Simmer consommé, white wine, split green peas, fresh or frozen peas, and lime juice for 10 minutes.

Combine chopped green onions, celery, green pepper, mushrooms, and garlic. Sauté in the olive oil until tender, then add to soup. Add herbs. Cover and simmer until split peas are tender — for about 1 hour. Discard bay leaf and coriander. Purée soup in a blender, adding sour cream and Roquefort cheese. Return to saucepan and add chopped green onion stalks, diced green pepper, chopped celery, green peas, marijuana, and sherry. Cover and simmer for 15 minutes.

Serve with chilled *vinho verde*.

Serves 8 to 10

Guinea Fowl with Wild Rice and Cream of Artichoke Heart Sauce for Larisa

1	large or 2 small guinea fowl heart and liver of the fowl
2 Tbsp (25mL)	olive oil
3	peppercorns
½ tsp (2mL)	tarragon
2 Tbsp (25mL)	dry Jerez sherry
1 cup (250mL)	cooked wild rice
6	unblanched almonds, crushed
3 Tbsp (40mL)	pine nuts
3	dried apricots, finely chopped
half a	green apple, chopped
2 Tbsp (25mL)	raisins
2	green onions, chopped
4	strips bacon
1	lemon, cut in slices
½ cup (125mL)	Calvados

Sauce

1	can "Bon Vivant" artichoke bisque
½ 14-ounce (398-mL)	can of artichoke hearts
2 Tbsp (25mL)	commercial sour cream
2 tsp (10mL)	chopped parsley
½ tsp (2mL)	dill
1 tsp (5mL)	tarragon

Wash the cavity of the guinea fowl and dry with paper towels. Sauté heart and liver in olive oil until cooked but still pink in the middle. Cool. Grind into a paste with peppercorns, tarragon, and sherry.

Combine with wild rice, nuts, fruits, and green onions to make a stuffing. Fill the cavity and sew up the opening. Place bacon strips across breast and cover with lemon slices.

Bake at 350°F (180°C) for 1 to 1¼ hours, depending on size, basting frequently. Add Calvados to basting juice as it collects in the bottom of the pan.

To make the sauce, combine ingredients in a blender and purée until smooth. Transfer to a small saucepan and heat through.

To serve, remove bacon and lemon slices. Cut the guinea fowl in half, dividing stuffing evenly. Serve with artichoke heart sauce.

Accompany with steamed asparagus in season, a light salad, and chilled Meursault wine.

Serves 2

Francis Coutellier

Francis Coutellier may be found at the University of Moncton, where he teaches in the visual arts department, or at his Shediac cottage — or on someone's boat where he's more than likely the head chef!

And he is probably cooking fish — scallops with Pernod, barbecued lobster, smoked herring, or mussels in wine. "I have my own smoker," he says, "for which I import sawdust from British Columbia. Isn't that marvellous? All the way across the continent from British Columbia to New Brunswick. It's worth it, though, because it really is the best.

"I cook all the time, both for my family and for guests. I love having people around me that I can cook for. And I love doing special table decorations. It's like building my assemblages. Once I took a big, bulging beef heart and I covered it with jello and then I made a lot of other smaller-shaped coloured jellies, which I placed all over the table. So the guests got to eat the centrepiece!

"I never cook from a book. I am always experimenting and trying something new. For me, cooking is intuitive. I cook because, for me, it's the same as the creative art in my life. That's one of the reasons why I don't like making desserts. With desserts, so often it is necessary to measure ingredients and use the scales, but that's not intuitive so I don't do them very often.

"I have composed a bilingual poem on how I would create a super sandwich. The lowest layer of it is very cheap, and it increases in price as you work your way to the top."

Progression et accumulations des valeurs
Progression and accumulations of values

Sur le pain vous calfeutrez de la margarine
On the margarine spread a bit of peanut butter
Sur le beurre d'arachide vous ramollissez du cheez whiz
On the cheez whiz throw on a bit of jam
Sur la confiture vous garnissez de tomates
On the tomatoes sprinkle grated hard-boiled eggs
Sur les oeufs durs vous roulez du jambon
On the ham slap on boned turkey breast
Sur les blancs de dinde vous lancez du poulet
On the chicken layer some garlic sausage slices
Sur les rondelles de saucisson à l'ail vous éparpillez du poisson à l'escavêche
On the fish *à l'escavêche* pile on some pepper steak
Sur le steak au poivre vous flambez le filet mignon
On the filet mignon lavish rabbit pâté
Sur le pâté de lapin vous roulez des pétoncles
On the scallops decorate with lobster tails
Sur les queues de homard, vous semez des crevettes louisianaises
On the Louisiana shrimps drop a few lemoned oysters
Sur les hûitres citronnées, vous laissez nager des truites au bleu
On the *truites au bleu* sprinkle Russian caviar
Sur le caviar russe vous entrelacez les cuisses de grenouilles
Crown the frogs' legs with foie gras truffled and laced with cognac

Francis Coutellier 1978
Frank Knifemaker 1978

Rabbit Pâté

1 3-pound (1.5-kg)	rabbit
1 3-pound (1.5-kg)	pork loin rib roast
	water
1	garlic clove, crushed
1 tsp (5mL)	salt
	freshly ground pepper
1 tsp (5mL)	thyme
1 tsp (5mL)	savory
1 tsp (5mL)	chopped parsley
2	bay leaves
½ cup (125mL)	white wine
½ cup (125mL)	cognac
½ cup (125mL)	rabbit stock
	pork fat or bacon slices
3	bay leaves

Pastry

1¾ cups (425mL)	flour
¼ tsp (1mL)	salt
¼ cup (50mL)	butter
¼ cup (50mL)	lard
2	egg yolks
¼ cup (50mL)	ice water (approx.)

Remove meat from rabbit and pork loin. There should be approximately 1¼ pounds (625g) of each. Cover rabbit carcass with water in saucepan and boil for 1½ hours to make stock. Cut rabbit and pork meat in strips and place in a shallow pan. Sprinkle with garlic and herbs. Add bay leaves, wine, cognac and ½ cup (125mL) rabbit stock. Cover and set in a cool place for 8 hours, stirring occasionally. Remove bay leaves and discard. Grind other ingredients together in a meat grinder or food processor.

To make pastry, combine flour and salt. Cut in butter and lard with a pastry blender or 2 knives until the mixture resembles coarse meal. Stir in egg yolks and ice water to form a smooth dough. Wrap in waxed paper and chill for 30 minutes.

Line the bottom and sides (which should be removable) of a rectangular 2-quart (2-L) pâté mold with thin strips of pork fat or bacon slices. Spread ground meat mixture evenly in pan. Press firmly into corners. Place 3 bay leaves on top.

Roll pastry to ½-inch (1-cm) thickness and cover pâté mold. Seal edges firmly to rim of mold.

Place in a *bain marie* of hot water and cook at 350°F (180°C) for 2 hours. Turn off heat, partly open oven door and allow pâté to cool in oven. When cool, remove from oven and weigh down with heavy bricks or cans wrapped in foil. Chill for 2 days before serving. To serve, remove sides of pan and place pâté on cutting board. Cut into slices ½ inch (1cm) thick.

Oysters in Champagne

6	oysters per person
	champagne
	crème fraîche (see page 65)
	chopped parsley

Open oysters and pour off liquid. Set oyster meat in deeper shell half and carefully pour in champagne. Top each oyster with a dollop of *crème fraîche*.

Set on a baking pan and bake at 400°F (200°C) for 3 minutes. Sprinkle with chopped parsley.

Serve as a first course with dark rye bread and unsalted butter.

Scallops with Pernod

2 pounds (1kg)	scallops
¼ cup (50mL)	butter
2	garlic cloves, crushed
¼ cup (50mL)	finely chopped parsley
½ tsp (2mL)	salt
	freshly ground pepper
1 cup (250mL)	Pernod, warmed
½ cup (125mL)	*crème fraîche* mixed with 1 Tbsp (15mL) flour

Crème fraîche

1 pint (500mL)	whipping cream
½ pint (250mL)	commercial sour cream

To make *crème fraîche*, combine creams in a small bowl. Cover loosely and let sit at room temperature for about 8 hours or until thick. Stir well. Cover tightly and store in refrigerator.

Rinse scallops under running cold water, drain in a colander, and dry thoroughly with paper towels. Melt butter in a large frying pan. Add garlic, parsley, salt, and pepper. Add scallops and sauté for about 5 minutes. Ignite warmed Pernod and pour over scallops. Then quickly stir in *crème fraîche* mixture.

Serve on a bed of rice. Top with a sprinkling of parsley.

Serves 4

Varnished Barbecued Lobster

2	lobsters, split in half lengthwise
½ cup (125mL)	melted butter
2	garlic cloves, crushed

Remove the tamale and roe from the lobsters and combine with the melted butter and crushed garlic. Keep warm.

Grill lobster halves, meat side down, over charcoal on a barbecue or hibachi for 10 to 15 minutes, taking care not to burn the shell. When cooked, turn meat side up and brush liberally with butter mixture.

Serves 2

Beef Heart: An Edible Centrepiece

1	beef heart
2 quarts (2L)	water
1 tsp (5mL)	thyme
1 tsp (5mL)	salt
1 tsp (5mL)	chopped parsley
¼ tsp (1mL)	paprika
1	bay leaf
2	onions, cut in quarters
2	carrots, sliced
2	stalks celery
	Jello — see below

Wash heart well, remove fat, arteries, veins, and blood. Soak in cold water for 1 hour.

Simmer 2 quarts (2L) water, spices, and vegetables for 30 minutes and then add heart. Cover and simmer for 2 to 3 hours or until heart is tender. Remove heart from broth, allow to cool, then chill.

Prepare Jello in several colours: yellow, red, orange, green. Chill Jello until it begins to thicken. Set heart in a shallow dish and arrange Jello artistically around and on top of the heart. Chill before displaying.

David Craven

Notorious among his friends for his eating habits, Toronto painter David Craven is a junk-food freak. "But I have my standards," he says. "I like to order in or pick up the stuff at the take-out joint and eat it at home. And I never use their serviettes. I definitely prefer to use my own."

David never eats breakfast or lunch. But he consumes gallons of coffee made in an overworked and broken-down coffee maker.

Although his wife is a home economics graduate, she is, claims David, his co-addict to the hot dogs and hamburgers at Harvey's. "But don't get me wrong. While we thrive on junk food, we like eating in nice restaurants too. It's the whole 'restaurant experience' and the ambience — being part of a congenial group — that I like best about restaurant eating, however, not really the food.

"In the winter time, when I'm painting day and night in my studio, I'll order in Swiss Chalet chicken every day. It's great because they deliver. I never get around to throwing out the empty containers so pretty soon there are stacks of empty Swiss Chalet boxes all over the place. It gets so bad I finally have to sweep them out to make room for more."

David has two "specialties" that he reluctantly admits to cooking, until now guarding this information in fear that public knowledge of it will ruin his reputation.

Specialty number one is Pepperidge Farm turnovers ("I love them, so I obviously have to cook them, right?"), particularly the ones with the raspberry filling.

"You're supposed to take them right out of the freezer and bake them just like the package says, only I don't because our freezer doesn't work too well, and they're generally partly thawed. So I just cook them less than you're supposed to.

"I'll eat them with a dessert fork, and maybe some vanilla ice cream, but I like them plain just as well. Mind you, I particularly love eating them with a bottle of chilled Chablis. It's really elegant. I can eat a whole box of them myself. At the end, I feel really sick; they just linger in your stomach, sort of like eating five bags of jujubes all at once."

His second specialty is popcorn. It hasn't a gourmet touch to it at all, but it's his way of doing it, and David says it's spartan because that's the way he likes it.

Spartan Popcorn

Spread a thin layer of oil in the bottom of a heavy saucepan and heat it until it begins to smoke. Pour in enough popcorn kernels to cover the bottom of the pan and put on the lid. Shake the pan back and forth over the heat until all the kernels have popped. Pour into a bowl and sprinkle with salt. Do not use any butter, margarine or oil on Spartan Popcorn because then it won't be spartan!

Alex Colville, *Refrigerator,* 1977. Acrylic polymer emulsion on board, 120 cm × 74.2 cm. Private collection.

Greg Curnoe

Greg and Sheila Curnoe's home sits on a large lot in central London. It has trees and open spaces, a hill, Greg's studio, a wine cellar, and a new garden adjoining a recent addition to the house.

The new garden is tucked behind a high wood fence — a lush arrangement of herbs, vegetables, a bubbling lily pond, and a picnic table where the Curnoes and their three children can eat alfresco.

"Having children really modifies your style of cooking," says Sheila Curnoe, "but we grow our own vegetables and herbs because we like to have them fresh at our fingertips. We can just walk out the door and pick them."

"One summer when we rented a cottage at Port Stanley," recalls Greg, "we ate only locally grown food — things like Lake Erie perch which we'd pan fry in butter, fresh corn, local strawberries, and so on. They were the best meals in the world because everything was so fresh."

While Sheila takes care of the fancy meals, Greg has his specialties.

"The kids love a dip I do. I crush four or five garlic cloves and whip them into a quart of yoghurt. It's superb yoghurt — Keffir — and made from whole milk. Then we all dip pita bread or raw vegetables in it."

"Greg also does great breakfast pancakes," Sheila says, "and once we had a real run on sugar pies. Greg had been in Quebec, painting, and when he came home, he made one sugar pie after another. We were eating them for breakfast, lunch, and dinner. I had to ask him to stop."

Hummus

2 cups (500mL)	cooked chick peas
1 tsp (5mL)	salt
3	garlic cloves, crushed
½ cup (125mL)	olive oil
¼ cup (50mL)	freshly squeezed lemon juice
2 Tbsp (25mL)	chopped parsley
2 Tbsp (25mL)	chopped fresh mint leaves

Put all ingredients in a blender or food processor. Blend at high speed until smooth. Serve as a dip with raw vegetables or pita bread.

Yield: 2 cups

Chicken Bordeaux

2	small chickens
½ cup (125mL)	flour
1 tsp (5mL)	salt
	freshly ground pepper
½ cup (125mL)	vegetable oil
1 cup (250mL)	canned tomatoes, drained
¼ cup (50mL)	flour mixed with ½ cup (125mL) water
1½ cups (375mL)	dry white wine
1	garlic clove, crushed
1 dozen	mushrooms

Cut chickens into quarters. Wash and dry thoroughly. Combine flour, salt, and pepper in a small bag. Shake chicken pieces in flour to coat evenly.

Heat oil in a large frying pan, and sauté chicken pieces until golden. Cover and cook over low heat for 30 minutes. Drain liquid from pan. Add tomatoes and bring to the boil. Stir in flour and water mixture. Add wine, garlic, and mushrooms, and stir until thickened. Cover and simmer for 15 minutes.

Serve with hot rice or noodles.

Serves 6

Wild Rice

1 cup (250mL)	wild rice
4 cups (1L)	water
1 tsp (5mL)	salt
4 Tbsp (50mL)	butter
1 cup (250mL)	sliced mushrooms
1 cup (250mL)	diced celery

Rinse rice under running cold water. Drain well. Bring salted water to the boil. Add rice. Cover and boil gently for 35 to 40 minutes.

Meanwhile, heat butter in a heavy frying pan. Sauté sliced mushrooms and celery until tender.

Drain rice. Toss with sautéed vegetables.

Serves 4

Poppy Seed Cake

½ cup (125mL)	poppy seeds
¾ cup (175mL)	boiling water
2 cups (475mL)	flour
1 Tbsp (15mL)	baking powder
¼ tsp (1mL)	baking soda
½ tsp (2mL)	salt
1½ cups (375mL)	sugar
6	eggs, separated
½ tsp (2mL)	cream of tartar
½ cup (125mL)	vegetable oil
2 tsp (10mL)	vanilla

Pour boiling water over the poppy seeds, cover, and let stand overnight.

Sift together into a large bowl the flour, baking powder, baking soda, salt, and sugar.

Beat egg whites with cream of tartar until soft peaks form.

Beat egg yolks slightly, add oil and vanilla and stir into dry ingredients. Beat until smooth, then fold in egg whites. Pour into an ungreased angel food pan. Bake at 325°F (160°C) for 60 to 70 minutes, or until springy.

Ukrainian Honey Cake

1 cup (250mL)	honey
½ cup (125mL)	butter
1 cup (250mL)	brown sugar
4	eggs, separated
3 cups (750mL)	flour
2 tsp (10mL)	baking soda
½ tsp (2mL)	baking powder
½ tsp (2mL)	salt
1 tsp (5mL)	cinnamon
1 cup (250mL)	commercial sour cream
½ cup (125mL)	chopped nuts
½ cup (125mL)	raisins

Boil honey and cool to room temperature. Cream butter and add sugar slowly, beating until light and fluffy. Add egg yolks one at a time. Beat in honey.

Sift together flour, baking soda, baking powder, salt, and cinnamon. Stir into butter mixture alternately with sour cream. Add nuts and raisins. Fold in stiffly beaten egg whites.

Pour into a greased bundt pan. Bake at 325°F (160°C) for 1 hour. Cool before turning out onto a wire rack.

Blender Pots de Crème

6 ounces (170g)	semi-sweet chocolate pieces
¾ cup (170mL)	milk, scalded
1	egg
2 Tbsp (25mL)	sugar
2 Tbsp (25mL)	brandy

Combine all ingredients in container of a blender. Blend at high speed for 1 minute. Pour into 4 custard cups or *pots de crème* dishes. Chill for at least 3 hours.

Serves 4

Nellie Curnoe's Rhubarb Pie

Pastry

5½ cups (1.25L)	flour
2 tsp (10mL)	salt
1 pound (454g)	lard
1	egg, slightly beaten
1 Tbsp (15mL)	vinegar
	water

Filling

4 cups (1L)	diced strawberry rhubarb
1 cup (250mL)	granulated sugar
1 Tbsp (15mL)	flour

Make pastry by sifting dry ingredients together. Cut in lard with a pastry blender or 2 knives until mixture resembles coarse meal. Put egg and vinegar into a 1-cup (250-mL) measure. Add enough water to bring the level up to the 1-cup (250-mL) mark. Add to flour, stirring to form a smooth dough. Divide in half, wrap in waxed paper and chill for 30 minutes before rolling out.

Combine filling ingredients.

Roll out half of pastry. Line a 9-inch (1-L) pie plate and pour in filling. Top with second piece of rolled out pastry. Trim to fit, moisten edges and crimp to seal. With a sharp knife cut several slits in top crust to let steam escape. Brush with milk.

Bake at 450°F (230°C) for 10 minutes. Reduce heat to 350°F (180°C) and bake for a further 30 minutes.

Louis de Niverville

Professing that his own cooking doesn't interest him very much, Louis de Niverville says, "I depend on friends who are good cooks to keep me supplied.

"I must admit I am very critical of food," he says. "Mostly I like things that are simply prepared, not overly spicy but, on the other hand, not bland.

"I'm always waiting for that extra special something to turn up. I like to be surprised by the exceptional. Fancy restaurants bother me because I always feel I'm being cheated in having to pay so much for what I get.

"I have this fantastic sense of security when I get a good meal, too. For me, that's really living."

There were thirteen children in the de Niverville family when Louis was growing up, and he learned as a child to like only fresh foods. "My mother was, and still is, a great cook, and I learned from her, I guess.

"I suppose it's a holdover, but today, I like, and will only cook, the freshest foods. I won't eat tomatoes in the winter because who knows when they were picked. I grow my own vegetables in the summer and shop at one of the Toronto markets. I don't like anything reheated a second time, not even stews or soups.

"Actually, even though I say my own cooking doesn't interest me, I still do cook."

Louis' Leek Soup

3 cups (750mL)	chicken stock
4	leeks, white part only, cut in julienne strips
2	cooked potatoes
1 bunch	celery leaves, chopped
½ cup (125mL)	whipping cream

Bring stock to a boil. Add leeks and simmer, covered, for 5 minutes.

Meanwhile, sieve the cooked potatoes or pass them through a potato ricer. Add to stock along with chopped celery leaves. Simmer for a further 5 minutes.

Stir in whipping cream and heat through but do not boil.

Serves 4

Celery Root Salad with Walnuts

1	large celery root
	water
1 Tbsp (15mL)	lemon juice
1 cup (250mL)	freshly shelled walnuts
	Green Mayonnaise

Peel celery root and grate. Soak grated root in a bowl of water to which lemon juice has been added.

At serving time, drain well and pat celery dry with paper towels. Toss with walnuts. Combine with enough green mayonnaise to bind together.

Serves 4

Green Mayonnaise

1	egg
1 Tbsp (15mL)	vinegar
1 Tbsp (15mL)	lemon juice
1 tsp (5mL)	brown sugar
1 Tbsp (15mL)	dry mustard
½ tsp (2mL)	salt
¼ tsp (1mL)	pepper
1 cup (250mL)	olive oil
1 cup (250mL)	chopped parsley or the leaves of 1 bunch of watercress, chopped

Place the egg, vinegar, lemon juice, brown sugar, mustard, salt, pepper, and ¼ cup (50mL) of the olive oil in a blender. Blend at high speed for a few seconds, then remove lid and very slowly add remaining olive oil in a thin, steady stream until mixture has thickened.

Add chopped parsley or watercress leaves and blend until mayonnaise turns a smooth green colour.

Yield: 1½ cups

Louis de Niverville, *In Hope of Spring*, 1979. Acrylic
with air brush on canvas, 91.4 cm × 106.7 cm.
Collection of John and Susan Potts, Toronto. Photo:
VIDA/Saltmarche, Toronto.

Rum Baba

1 tsp (5mL)	sugar
¼ cup (50mL)	warm water
1 package	yeast
2 cups (500mL)	flour
4	eggs, lightly beaten
½ tsp (2mL)	salt
1 Tbsp (15mL)	sugar
⅔ cup (175mL)	soft unsalted butter
1 Tbsp (15mL)	dried currants
	fresh strawberries

Rum Syrup

1 cup (250mL)	sugar
1¼ cups (300mL)	water
¾ cup (175mL)	rum

Crème Chantilly

1 cup (250mL)	whipping cream
2 Tbsp (25mL)	sifted confectioners sugar
1 tsp (5mL)	vanilla

To make the rum baba, in a small bowl, dissolve the sugar in warm water. Add the yeast. Let stand 10 minutes then stir.

Sift flour in a large bowl. Make a well in the centre and pour in the lightly beaten eggs and the yeast mixture. Stir, gradually incorporating flour, then knead in the bowl for 3 to 5 minutes. Cover with a clean towel and let rise in a warm place until double in bulk — approximately 1½ hours.

Punch dough down. Add salt and sugar and knead some more in the bowl. Add butter and currants, mixing together until well blended.

Grease a baba tin and fill with dough. Cover with a towel and let rise until double in bulk, approximately 1½ hours.

Bake at 450°F (230°C) for 10 minutes. Reduce heat to 350°F (180°C) and bake for a further 20 to 25 minutes.

While the baba is baking, make the Rum Syrup by boiling sugar and water together for 10 minutes. Remove from heat, stir in rum, and set aside.

Turn baba out of mold onto a wire rack set over a tray and slowly drench with Rum Syrup.

To make the Crème Chantilly, whip cream until stiff. Fold in sugar and vanilla.

Serve with strawberries soaked in a little of the Rum Syrup and with Crème Chantilly.

Cheesecake

	butter
½ cup (125mL)	graham cracker crumbs
2 pounds (1kg)	cream cheese, at room temperature
4	eggs
1¾ cups (425mL)	granulated sugar
¼ cup (50mL)	lemon juice
2 tsp (10mL)	grated lemon rind
1 tsp (5mL)	vanilla

Butter well an 8-inch (1.5-L) springform pan. Press the graham cracker crumbs well into the sides and bottom of the pan.

Place remaining ingredients in large bowl of electric mixer. Start beating at low speed and, as the ingredients mix together, increase the speed to high, scraping the sides of the bowl constantly with a rubber spatula. Continue beating until mixture is smooth.

Pour into prepared pan and shake gently to level the mixture. Set the pan in a slightly bigger pan in which there is sufficient hot water to reach halfway up the sides of the cake pan.

Bake at 325°F (160°C) for 2 hours. Turn off heat and let cake sit in oven for a further one hour. Cool on a rack before serving. Garnish with fruit or berries if desired.

Jacques de Tonnancour

"I'm not very adventurous about food," says painter Jacques de Tonnancour, even though his world travels have taken him to far-flung areas of gastronomic curiosities. Turtle steak seems to be about the limit of his experimentation, although he has been in places where others ate filet of boa, crocodile-tail steaks, and monkey roasted on a spit.

Food is less exotic in his Montreal home. "Joan does most of the cooking," Jacques says. "I do it for fun, generally just for the two of us, but sometimes if we're entertaining I'll also cook. Every now and again I'll do something like *boeuf bourguignonne.* I don't know the classic recipe for it, so each time I have to re-invent it.

"It would kill all my satisfaction to have to follow directions. I like to improvise because for me, that is knowledge, exploration, and discovery. But to give or follow directions is to cut off creativity.

"For this reason, it is difficult for me to pass on recipes. For instance, this past weekend I had six chicken breasts. I prepared four of them one way and two another because I couldn't fit all six into the pan at once. These things are never set. I didn't know this would happen so it was a good thing I wasn't following any specific instructions. I could never do it exactly the same way again either, and I wouldn't want to.

"I could never be a professional chef because a chef must have constant standards. He must establish a continuity so that from day to day his patrons know that if they order a particular dish, it's going to taste a particular way—the same way, say, that it tasted when they last had it. I could never live this way."

Avocado Dessert

3 avocados
juice of 1 large lime
sugar to taste

Scoop pulp from avocados and mash with lime juice and sugar to taste. Spoon back into 4 avocado shells, mounding it attractively.

Serves 4

Paterson Ewen

Paterson Ewen, in his modest way, describes himself as a "rather ordinary cook."

"What I do best," he says, "is pressure-cooker cooking. It's very fast and very good, and the food comes out pure and natural with all its nutrition still intact." Pat likes pressure-cookers so much, he has two of them so he can do a variety of things all at once.

"I'll mix things like pork chops and vegetables in the same pot and it's good enough to serve to guests. I'll also pressure-cook roasts, chickens, *coq au vin* or a shoulder of pork and most vegetables."

Pat now paints and teaches in London. He has always had an interest in food, and recollects that as a child he liked to watch his mother working in their Montreal kitchen. "She used *The Boston Cookbook* and made some wonderful things like King Edward Sauce. I can still remember some of the delicious smells of things she baked — pies, Christmas cakes, and tea biscuits. I also had a Scottish aunt who lived outside Montreal. At her place, there was always a huge pot simmering on her wood stove and we called it 'Aunt Annie's Soup.'

"My four sons, who are all grown up now, are interested in food, too. The eldest, now thirty-one, is keen on gourmet cooking. At the age of twelve, he'd order brains in restaurants and surprise the waiters."

Recently, Pat shed thirty pounds in less than five months "by cutting out carbohydrates, alcohol, and beer! I've come to the conclusion that it isn't what you put in your mouth, it's how much. You could eat chocolate ice cream every day but as long as it's a little, you'd still lose weight."

Pressure-Cooker Coq au vin

3 pounds (1.5 kg)	chicken pieces
	flour
2 Tbsp (25 mL)	butter
1	garlic clove, crushed
¼ tsp (1 mL)	thyme
1 Tbsp (15 mL)	chopped parsley
½	bay leaf
6	large mushrooms, sliced
½ cup (125 mL)	dry red wine
	salt and pepper

Wash and dry chicken pieces. Dredge with flour. Heat butter in a 5-quart (5-L) pressure cooker. Brown chicken pieces. Add remaining ingredients except salt and pepper. Close cover securely. Follow directions of pressure-cooker manual and cook for 10 minutes with pressure regulator rocking slowly. Set aside for 15 to 20 minutes, to let pressure drop, then uncover. Add salt and pepper to taste.

Serves 6

Pressure-Cooker Lamb Stew

3 pounds (1.5 kg)	lamb, cut in 1-inch (2.5-cm) cubes
2 Tbsp (25 mL)	butter
1	green pepper, diced
6	onions, coarsely chopped
1 Tbsp (15 mL)	Worcestershire sauce
6	carrots, cut in half
¾ cup (175 mL)	hot water
	salt and pepper

Heat butter in a 5-quart (5-L) pressure-cooker and brown the lamb cubes. Add remaining ingredients except salt and pepper. Close cover securely. Follow directions of pressure-cooker manual and cook for 10 minutes with pressure regulator rocking slowly. Set aside for 15 to 20 minutes to let pressure drop, then uncover. Add salt and pepper to taste.

Serves 6

Broiled Steak

	sirloin steak, 1 inch (2.5 cm) thick
1	garlic clove, cut in slivers

Remove steak from refrigerator at least two hours before serving. With a sharp knife, cut several small slits in meat. Insert garlic slivers in slits. Preheat broiler. Set steak on a rack, 4 inches (10 cm) from heat, and broil at high heat for 7 minutes on one side. Turn over and broil for a further 3 minutes for medium steaks. Adjust time for rare or well-done steaks.

Save juice to pour over meat. Cut in half and serve on 2 heated plates.

Serves 2

Photo: Michaelin McDermott, Winnipeg Art Gallery

Ivan Eyre

Ivan and Brenda Eyre lead a life that could best be described as calm, unhurried, friendly, and very much attuned to nature. Their modern multi-level home nestles on a wooded lot that slopes down to Winnipeg's LaSalle River. Wild raspberries and Saskatoonberry bushes run through their backyard woods.

"We both grew up in small prairie towns," says Ivan. "I clearly remember the taste and feel of unpasteurized honey in my mouth. When we were children, both our mothers served plain, simple foods, even though they came from mid-European countries and knew how to prepare their traditional cuisines. But both Brenda's father and mine liked the simple things best.

"I remember, though, as a child, going through a period of baking Parkins every afternoon," recalls Ivan. "They're wonderful molasses cookies — crunchy with rolled oats — dark brown and delicious. They must have been one of my first culinary ventures."

Nowadays, mealtime at the Eyres' is a family activity involving their two teenaged sons. "That's a very important time of the day for us. At dinner, we all sit around the dining room table and talk a lot together. We might have a glass of wine, and often we put some background music on the stereo. The children enjoy it, and it gives us all a chance to keep in touch with one another."

Like many people today, the Eyres' taste preferences are moving away from meat towards a more vegetarian approach to eating. "We would really rather not eat meat," says Brenda, "but the boys insist on having it." She has recently begun experimenting with health-food recipes — often adapting some of her old favourites by exchanging ingredients — and has found that not only have the results been exciting and pleasing, but she's enjoying cooking more.

The appearance and feel of food are important to the Eyres. Ivan dislikes spongy cakes that spring back when bitten into — the texture bothers him. Brenda has discovered that breading liver in whole-wheat crumbs improves both its appearance and texture.

When Brenda puts together a dish, she takes into account the compositional arrangements of the foods on the plates. The Eyres have a collection of serving dishes that they have picked up on world travels, which enhance the presentation of their meals.

Brenda's Meat Loaf

2 pounds (1kg)	ground beef
1 cup (250mL)	bran
1 cup (250mL)	bulghur
½ cup (125mL)	whole wheat bread crumbs
2	garlic cloves, crushed
2	large carrots, grated
2	stalks celery, chopped
1	medium onion, chopped
2 tsp (10mL)	sea salt
1 tsp (5mL)	cumin
¼ tsp (1mL)	freshly ground pepper
½ tsp (2mL)	ground rose hips
1 Tbsp (15mL)	sage
¼ cup (50mL)	chopped parsley
4	eggs
½ cup (125mL)	milk

Mix all ingredients together. Pat into two lightly greased standard loaf pans. Bake at 300°F (150°C) for 2½ hours.

Yield: 2 loaves

Parkins

½ cup (125mL)	butter
½ cup (125mL)	dark brown sugar
1	egg
½ cup (125mL)	molasses
1½ cups (375mL)	whole wheat flour
½ tsp (2mL)	cinnamon
½ tsp (2mL)	nutmeg
½ tsp (2mL)	ginger
1 tsp (5mL)	baking soda
1 cup (250mL)	rolled oats

Cream butter and sugar together until light and fluffy. Add the egg and continue to beat. Pour in molasses and mix together well.

In a separate bowl, sift together the flour, spices, and baking soda. Gradually add dry ingredients to the butter mixture and when thoroughly combined, add the rolled oats.

Drop teaspoonfuls onto a greased baking pan, leaving 3 inches (8cm) between each cookie.

Bake at 350°F (180°C) for 8 to 10 minutes, taking care that the Parkins do not burn.

Yield: 4 dozen

Whole Wheat Brownies

1 cup (250mL)	whole wheat flour
2 cups (500mL)	wheat germ
1 cup (250mL)	powdered milk
½ tsp (2mL)	sea salt
1 tsp (5mL)	baking powder
½ cup (125mL)	cocoa
2 cups (500mL)	lightly packed brown sugar
1 cup (250mL)	coffee
3 tsp (15mL)	vanilla
4	eggs, beaten
¾ cup (175mL)	vegetable oil
3 Tbsp (40mL)	dark molasses
1 tsp (5mL)	grated grapefruit rind
1 cup (250mL)	unsweetened coconut
½ cup (125mL)	walnuts

In a large bowl mix together the flour, wheat germ, powdered milk, salt, baking powder, cocoa, and sugar.

Add the liquid ingredients and combine thoroughly. Stir in the grapefruit rind, coconut, and walnuts.

Pour into 2 greased 9-inch (1.5-L) square pans. Bake at 350°F (180°C) for 30 minutes. Allow to cool on a rack before turning out of pans.

Ivan Eyre, *Studio Lunch,* 1971. Oil on canvas, 31 cm
× 36.5 cm. Collection of the artist.

Joe Fafard

When Joe Fafard was an art student, he lived in a boarding house in a room that came equipped with a hot plate. "Fortunately I wasn't that concerned about eating," he says, "or I'd have been pretty discouraged. Then I 'batched' it for a couple of years and almost starved to death. And, you know, I don't really have any extra pounds that I can afford to lose."

Now that he is married, he is still slim in spite of his wife Susan's cooking, which leans heavily on the traditional Mennonite recipes from her background.

The Fafards live outside Regina where Joe sculpts and creates his ceramic figures in the small prairie town of Pense. They have their own vegetable patch and they eat well. "I don't take a very serious interest in preparing food," admits Joe, "but Susan is a great cook.

"We have three kids between the ages of nine and thirteen so we don't get around to eating anything fancy," he says. "We hate hamburger joints. We like to eat good food, well prepared, and attractively served. But I guess we're habit eaters, mostly because of the kids."

Photo: Cal Bailey

Holubschi
Stuffed Cabbage Leaves

1 cup (250mL)	rice
1	large cabbage
2 Tbsp (25mL)	fat
1	onion, finely chopped
½ pound (250g)	ground beef
1 tsp (5mL)	salt
¼ tsp (1mL)	pepper
1 10-ounce (284-mL)	can tomato soup
½ cup (125mL)	commercial sour cream

Cook rice according to package directions. Set aside.

Remove 18 outer leaves from the cabbage and cook in a large pot of boiling salted water for about 5 minutes or until they are limp. Drain and cool.

Heat the fat in a heavy frying pan. Add onion and sauté until golden. Add ground beef, cooked rice, salt and pepper, and cook until meat is lightly browned.

Drop a large spoonful of meat mixture on the stem end of each cabbage leaf. Roll up, tucking in the ends and fasten with a toothpick. Place close together in a baking pan. Cover with undiluted tomato soup.

Bake at 350°F (180°C) for 45 minutes. Just before serving, swirl in sour cream.

Makes 18 cabbage rolls to serve 6

Borscht

4 cups (1L)	pork stock
2 cups (500mL)	beets, cut in julienne strips
½ cup (125mL)	diced carrots
1 cup (250mL)	shredded cabbage
½ cup (125mL)	diced potato
½ cup (125mL)	peas
1 cup (250mL)	tomato juice
1	medium onion, finely chopped
1 tsp (5mL)	salt
1	bay leaf
1	sprig of dill
½ tsp (2mL)	mixed spices
	commercial sour cream

Combine all ingredients except sour cream in a large saucepan and simmer, covered, for 30 minutes.

Serve in heated soup bowls topped with a dollop of sour cream.

Serves 8

Pumpkin Pie

2	eggs
¾ cup (175mL)	sugar
1 tsp (5mL)	cinnamon
½ tsp (2mL)	ginger
½ tsp (2mL)	nutmeg
½ tsp (2mL)	salt
¼ tsp (1mL)	mace
2 Tbsp (25mL)	flour
2 cups (500mL)	cooked pumpkin
½ cup (125mL)	cream
unbaked 9-inch (1-L)	pie shell

Beat eggs until light. Add sugar, spices, and flour and combine thoroughly. Stir in pumpkin and cream. Pour into unbaked pie shell.

Bake at 400°F (200°C) for 10 minutes. Reduce heat to 325°F (160°C) and bake for a further 40 minutes or until filling is firm.

Joe Fafard, *Papa Bull,* 1979. Clay, acrylic paint, glazes,
40 cm × 60 cm (approx.). Private collection.

Gathie Falk

Gathie Falk's Vancouver home always looks as if it is expecting the imminent arrival of guests. On one table is a pyramid of crimson apples, on another, a birthday cake, iced with gooey blue frosting. Fried chicken breasts and plump fish repose near each other. Elsewhere a bag of oranges sits on the floor and beyond is a plate of lemons.

Closer inspection reveals that neither the taste buds nor the stomach will be satiated by this scattered banquet, for it is but a visual feast resulting from Gathie's most recent sessions with clay and glazes.

Well known for her lively ceramics, Gathie Falk says, "For many years I've been inspired by what I saw around me — food, clothing, games, furniture. I like best to work with these subjects, and for a long time, food was my prime passion. It is a subject that everyone knows well. People eat all the time.

"Actually, I came to my interest in food rather far on in my life. When I was a child, my mother, who was a good cook, would make special things for us children like rolled-up crêpes, but we were never allowed to help in the kitchen.

"I used to make her angry, I fear, because she would call out to me from another room, 'Are the potatoes boiling?' and I'd answer her, 'The water is, but I don't know about the potatoes.'

"I always lived with my mother, but when I was in my mid-thirties, she became ill and was hospitalized, so I had to learn to cook for myself. Now I make a point, when I'm eating alone, of setting a proper table, maybe with a candle, otherwise one can become a savage about food.

"Today, I like reading cookbooks. Mostly I cook in a hurry, but I also like cooking good things once in a while. My friends enjoy my food, and often ask me to do special things for them. Then I'll pull out all the stops."

Photo: Robert Keziere

Pakistani Kima

2 Tbsp (25mL)	butter
1 cup (250mL)	chopped onion
1	garlic clove, crushed
1 pound (500g)	ground beef
2 Tbsp (25mL)	curry powder
1 tsp (5mL)	salt
¼ tsp (1mL)	pepper
½ tsp (2mL)	cinnamon
½ tsp (2mL)	ginger
½ tsp (2mL)	turmeric
1 19-ounce (540-mL)	can tomatoes
1 cup (250mL)	frozen peas
2	bananas, sliced
½ cup (125mL)	toasted coconut

Melt butter in a heavy frying pan. Sauté onion and garlic until golden. Add ground beef and brown, then stir in remaining ingredients, except bananas and coconut. Cover and simmer for 25 minutes.

Serve on a bed of rice, topped with sliced banana and toasted coconut.

Serves 3 or 4

Cheese Pie

Crust	
¾ cup (175mL)	flour
½ tsp (2mL)	salt
¼ tsp (1mL)	dry mustard
1 cup (250mL)	grated Cheddar cheese
¼ cup (50mL)	melted butter
Filling	
2 Tbsp (25mL)	butter
2 cups (500mL)	thinly sliced onion
1 cup (250mL)	cooked, drained noodles
2	eggs
1 cup (250mL)	hot milk
½ tsp (2mL)	salt
	freshly ground pepper
1 cup (250mL)	grated Cheddar cheese

To make the crust, sift together the flour, salt, and mustard. Stir in the grated cheese. Toss with melted butter. Press into the bottom and sides of a 9-inch (1-L) pie plate.

To make the filling, melt the butter in a heavy frying pan and sauté the onions until they are transparent. Add the noodles and mix together well. Spread evenly over the crust.

Beat eggs and slowly add milk. Stir in salt, pepper, and grated cheese. Pour into pie shell. Bake at 325°F (160°C) for 40 minutes or until custard is set.

Serves 4

Zucchini and Eggs

4	medium zucchini
	flour
2 Tbsp (25mL)	butter
2 Tbsp (25mL)	vegetable oil
2 tsp (10mL)	dried parsley flakes
1 tsp (5mL)	oregano
	salt and pepper
2	eggs, lightly beaten
1 Tbsp (15mL)	milk
2 Tbsp (25mL)	grated Parmesan cheese

Wash and dry the zucchini. Cut off the ends and discard. Cut the zucchini in half lengthwise, then in 1-inch (2.5-cm) pieces. Dip zucchini in flour, shaking to remove excess.

Heat butter and oil in a heavy 12-inch (3-L) frying pan. Add zucchini, sprinkle with parsley, oregano, salt, and pepper, and sauté until brown. Arrange zucchini evenly in frying pan.

Combine beaten eggs and milk and pour over zucchini. Cook slowly over medium heat until eggs are set. Sprinkle with Parmesan cheese. Loosen with a spatula and cut in wedges.

Serves 3

Wally and Bill and Gathie's "Everything" Casserole

2 pounds (1kg)	ground beef
1	garlic clove, crushed
1 tsp (5mL)	oregano
1 4-ounce (113-g)	can chili peppers, drained
1	green pepper, diced
1	large onion, diced
1 10-ounce (284-mL)	can mushrooms, drained
	salt and pepper
1 14-ounce (398-mL)	can tomato sauce
1 tsp (5mL)	sugar
1 pound (500g)	wide noodles, cooked
1 pound (500g)	sharp Cheddar cheese, grated
1 7-ounce (200-mL)	can kernel corn
1 4-ounce (113-g)	can pitted ripe olives, drained and sliced

Brown the ground beef well in a large frying pan. Pour off all fat that has accumulated except for 4 tablespoons (50mL). Remove meat to a bowl and set aside.

Brown garlic in remaining fat. Stir in oregano, chili peppers, green pepper, onion, mushrooms, and salt and pepper. Sauté until golden. Stir in tomato sauce and sugar. Return meat to frying pan and combine well. Cover the bottom of a casserole dish with a thin layer of the meat and tomato mixture. Spread a single layer of cooked noodles on top. Sprinkle with grated cheese, corn kernels, and some slices of olive. Repeat with another layer of meat sauce, and so on. Finish with a layer of meat sauce and a heavy sprinkling of cheese. Bake at 350°F (180°C) for 1 hour.

Serves 6

Scones

2 cups (475mL)	flour
4 tsp (20mL)	baking powder
½ tsp (2mL)	salt
¼ cup (50mL)	sugar
⅔ cup (175mL)	milk powder
¾ cup (175mL)	cold butter
¾ cup (175mL)	dried currants
⅔ cup (175mL)	water

Sift together the flour, baking powder, salt, sugar, and milk powder. Cut in butter with a pastry blender or 2 knives until mixture resembles coarse meal. Stir in currants. Quickly stir the water into the dry ingredients, adding a little more if necessary until the dough holds together. Pat dough into an 8-inch (20-cm) square. Cut into 2-inch (5-cm) square pieces.

Place on a greased baking pan. Bake at 425°F (220°C) for 10 to 12 minutes or until golden.

Yield: 16

Waffles

2 cups (500mL)	flour
4 tsp (20mL)	baking powder
¼ tsp (1mL)	salt
3	eggs, separated
1¾ cups (400mL)	milk
½ cup (125mL)	melted butter

Sift together the flour, baking powder, and salt. Beat egg yolks and gradually add milk. Add to flour mixture. Stir in melted butter.

Beat egg whites until stiff peaks form. Fold into flour mixture.

Spoon batter on lightly oiled waffle griddle. Close lid. Cook until crisp and golden brown.

Yield: 1 dozen waffles each 5 inches by 5 inches (12.5cm by 12.5cm)

Tom's Crêpes

1¼ cups (300mL)	milk
2	eggs
½ tsp (2mL)	salt
2 Tbsp (25mL)	vegetable oil
1 cup (250mL)	flour
	butter

Mix all ingredients, except butter, together in a blender. Cover and set aside for 2 hours before using.

Lightly butter a 6-inch (15-cm) crêpe pan, preferably Teflon-coated. Heat until butter foams. Pour in about ¼ cup (50mL) crêpe batter. Swirl around in pan to coat bottom evenly in a thin layer. Pour off excess. Cook over medium-high heat until crêpe is brown on bottom. Loosen with a spatula and flip over to cook the other side briefly. Turn out onto a wire rack and continue in the same manner with the remaining batter.

Serve with assorted condiments such as sugar and sliced lemon, fresh or frozen fruits, whipped cream, sour cream, cottage cheese, or a combination of any or all of these.

Yield: about 2 dozen 6-inch (15-cm) crêpes

Blintzes

	Filling
1½ cups (375mL)	dry cottage cheese
1	egg yolk
1 Tbsp (15mL)	soft butter
1 tsp (5mL)	vanilla or grated lemon rind
12 10-inch (25-cm)	crêpes cooked on one side only (see above)
	butter

Beat together all the filling ingredients until well mixed. Lay each crêpe cooked-side up, and place a large spoonful of filling in the centre. Fold over the edges to form an oblong envelope.

Heat a thin coating of butter in a heavy frying pan. Fry blintzes until golden on both sides. Serve warm.

Yield: 12 blintzes

Very Good Cake

1 package	yellow cake mix
1 package	instant lemon pudding
4	eggs
¾ cup (175mL)	vegetable oil
¾ cup (175mL)	white wine
1 tsp (5mL)	nutmeg

Beat all ingredients together with an electric mixer for 4 minutes. Pour into 2 greased and floured 9-inch (1.5-L) layer cake pans.

Bake at 350°F (180°C) for 35 to 40 minutes. Let cool before inverting onto a wire rack. Frost with favourite icing.

Joey's Recipe for Cheesecake

1 cup (250mL)	graham cracker crumbs
1 pound (454g)	cream cheese, at room temperature
4	egg yolks
¾ cup (175mL)	sugar
4 tsp (20mL)	flour
1 cup (250mL)	commercial sour cream
1 tsp (5mL)	grated lemon rind
1 tsp (5mL)	lemon juice
1 tsp (5mL)	vanilla
4	egg whites
¼ cup (50mL)	sugar

Butter an 8-inch (3-L) springform pan and press graham cracker crumbs into it.

Beat cream cheese until light and fluffy. Add egg yolks and continue beating until mixture is very smooth. Gradually add sugar and flour. Stir in sour cream, lemon rind, lemon juice, and vanilla.

Beat egg whites until stiff peaks form. Gradually add sugar. Fold into cream cheese mixture. Pour into prepared springform pan.

Bake at 300°F (150°C) for 70 minutes. Turn off oven and let cake cool in the oven with the door slightly open.

To serve, remove sides of pan. Cut into wedges and top with fresh strawberries or raspberries if desired.

Gathie Falk, *Picnic with Lemons,* 1977. Clay, glazes.
Collection of the Canada Council Art Bank. Photo:
Yvan Boulerice.

John Fox

John Fox was late in discovering food.

"My mother was a meat-and-potatoes kind of cook, but during my student days of painting in France and Italy, I really came to like food. Of all the European cuisines I know, I like Tuscan food best because its simplicity and freshness appeal to me. Only very young vegetables are used and they are cooked very little.

"Up until a couple of years ago, though, I still took food pretty much for granted, having always been taken care of and well fed. I was spoiled, I guess."

But then things changed. "I borrowed a copy of a Julia Child cookbook and set about learning how to cook. I didn't know a thing about heat before I started so I had a lot to learn. I had a two-burner hot plate in my studio and I decided to begin with omelettes, but Julia Child's method didn't work for me and I had to develop my own technique. I don't know how many eggs I went through in the process, but I still love omelettes and I enjoy a variety of fillings in them."

John has graduated from the hot plate to a handsome stove in his Montreal studio, but still considers his Napolitana coffee maker an essential kitchen utensil. For many years it was often featured in his paintings, and several times a day he takes great care in making a serious espresso in it.

"Coffee is very important to me," he says, "and I probably drink too much of it. I have such happy memories of being in Venice, standing at the counter of a tiny restaurant, rubbing elbows with Italian office workers, and breakfasting on a cup of espresso and a sweet paper-wrapped pastry. What a way to start the day!"

Kidneys in Mustard Sauce

4	veal kidneys
4 Tbsp (50mL)	butter
1	garlic clove, crushed
1 cup (250mL)	sliced mushrooms
1½ Tbsp (25mL)	Dijon-style mustard
½ tsp (2mL)	dry mustard
1 tsp (5mL)	tomato paste
1½ Tbsp (25mL)	flour
½ cup (125mL)	dry red wine
1 cup (250mL)	chicken stock
1	bay leaf
	salt and pepper to taste

Soak kidneys in cold salted water for 2 hours. Drain. Remove and discard white membrane. Chop kidneys into bite-sized pieces.

Heat butter in a heavy frying pan over medium-high heat. Sauté kidneys until brown. Remove and set aside. Add garlic to pan and sauté over low heat for 2 minutes. Stir in mushrooms and sauté, adding more butter if necessary. When golden, add Dijon-style mustard. Stir for 1 minute.

Remove pan from heat. Add dry mustard, tomato paste, and flour. Combine thoroughly, then add wine, stock, and bay leaf. Simmer 5 minutes. If too thick, add more stock.

Return kidneys to pan. Cover and simmer for 15 minutes. Add salt and pepper to taste.

Serves 4

Scaloppine al Limone

1½ pounds (750g)	veal scaloppine
	salt and pepper
	flour
2 Tbsp (25mL)	butter
2 Tbsp (25mL)	olive oil
¾ cup (175mL)	beef stock
6	thin lemon slices
1 Tbsp (15mL)	lemon juice

Sprinkle veal with salt and pepper. Dredge with flour, shaking to remove excess. Heat butter and oil in a heavy frying pan over medium heat. Brown veal on each side. Remove and set aside.

Pour ½ cup (125mL) of the stock into the frying pan. Boil for 2 minutes, scraping brown bits from sides and bottom of pan. Return veal to pan. Arrange lemon slices on top. Cover and simmer for 10 minutes. Remove veal and lemon. Add remaining ¼ cup (50mL) beef stock and boil, uncovered, until thickened. Stir in lemon juice.

To serve, layer scaloppine on a heated platter, pouring the sauce evenly over the veal.

Serves 4

Omelette for One

1 Tbsp (15mL)	butter
2	eggs
¼ tsp (1mL)	salt
	freshly ground pepper

Melt butter in an omelette pan set over medium-low heat.

Combine eggs, salt, and pepper with a fork. Pour into pan and let cook for a minute without stirring, then tilt pan and with a spatula, lift edges to permit runny egg to flow underneath. Continue until centre is custard-like.

Meanwhile, heat plate in oven. To remove omelette from pan, grasp plate in one hand and omelette pan in the other and tilt pan so that omelette rolls over on itself and out onto the plate.

Serves 1

David Gilhooly, *Donuts,* 1979. Clay and glazes, life-size.

Yves Gaucher

Behind Yves Gaucher's north Montreal studio is an enormous vegetable garden. And in the basement is a large wine cellar where Yves not only stores his thousands of bottles, but also presses his own grapes for fermenting and bottling. It's a very professional-looking operation.

"We enjoy wine, and the activity of making our own, so every year it becomes something of a festival down here," he says.

Cooking is important in the Gaucher family, with Yves assuming the role of master chef much of the time.

"My wife and I don't work together in the kitchen very well. She has her lousy way of working," he says with a twinkle in his eyes, "and I have my fantastic way so we don't do it together. I used to do all the cooking for the family when I was painting at home and my wife was working. She'd come home at night, and I'd say to her, 'You must have had a hard day; here, I'll get dinner for you.' "

The Gauchers like "interesting" food. "I do a fantastic dish made from fish and about six kinds of wild game. It's highly illegal, of course, but so good. There are partridge, pheasant, deer, moose, and other meats and fishes in it, and they're all marinated separately before being cooked together. I can't kill any of these things myself, but I love to cook and eat them.

"In Morocco, I was fed wild boar by a real gourmand. It was like nothing else I've ever tasted. When he came to Canada, I wanted to reciprocate by feeding him something special, so I cooked a whole salmon on the barbecue, turning it over every five minutes, and basting it with olive oil, wine, and almonds. It was equally fantastic.

"I have a superb recipe for green-turtle liver which I'll share. The basic ingredients are:
   1 DC-9 (or other) to Miami
   1 connecting Boeing 707 Southern Airways to Grand Cayman Island
   1 Honda Civic rented from Cico
        OR
   1 VW Thing from Coconut Car Rentals

"Drive out of Georgetown past Seven-Mile Beach towards Spanish Bay Reef and stop at the Cayman Turtle Farm. It is the only sea turtle farm in the world. On Monday and Thursday mornings, you can get fresh green-turtle steaks, for this is when they freeze them immediately after cutting them up. The liver cannot be frozen and does not keep at all in this very hot climate.

"Since the turtle-liver market is non-existent in Grand Cayman, and since the Caymanians are very hospitable, the foreman of the farm will gladly give, along with his favourite recipe, a full bag of fresh liver, without charge, to deserving *fourchettes* and lovable people.

"The taste of turtle liver is extremely fine, sort of half way between calf liver and calf brain in consistency. Therefore it has to be fried a bit longer than calf liver.

"Marinate it with two carrots, two onions, two spoonfuls of olive oil and some salt and pepper (and a bit of white wine) for about half an hour; bread it and fry it in a hot pan.

"I wish you the experience with a bottle of Meursault."

Lamb and Jugged Beaver

| 1 25-pound (10-kg) | young beaver, cut up |
| 2 | legs of lamb |

Marinade

2	carrots, sliced
1	bunch parsley
2	large onions, chopped
1 tsp (5mL)	thyme
1	garlic clove, crushed
2	bay leaves
6	peppercorns
½ cup (125mL)	cognac
	red wine
2 Tbsp (25mL)	olive oil

3	beef bouillon cubes
1 Tbsp (15mL)	cornstarch
	salt and pepper

Remove all fat from the beaver. Discard liver and other organs. Note that the meat along the spinal column, the front legs, and the tail are very good. Put beaver and lamb in a large shallow dish. Mix together all ingredients of marinade, with enough wine to be able to spoon it over the meat frequently during 4 days of marinating. Add to meat, and keep refrigerated during this time, basting the meat and turning it often.

Cook the meat and the marinade in a large pot, adding enough water to cover the meat completely. Simmer, covered, until lamb meat comes away from the bone—at least 2 hours. Remove lamb from the pot and continue cooking beaver for at least 4 hours or until meat is tender.

When done, remove beaver meat with a slotted spoon and combine with lamb. Remove all grease from cooking liquid and add 3 cups (750mL) boiling water to which 3 beef bouillon cubes have been added. Boil rapidly for 40 minutes. Strain into a smaller pot and add 1 tablespoon (15mL) cornstarch dissolved in 2 tablespoons (25mL) water. Stir until thickened. Pour over beaver and lamb meat. Taste for seasoning and add salt and pepper. Heat through before serving.

This will serve a large crowd, the numbers depending on the size of the beaver.

Note: This recipe has not been tested.

Jugged Hare

1	rabbit
½ pound (250g)	lean pork, diced
3	onions, diced
2 Tbsp (25mL)	flour
4 cups (1L)	red wine
1 Tbsp (15mL)	cognac
1	*bouquet garni*
20	small cooked mushrooms
20	small glazed onions

Marinade

3 Tbsp (40mL)	cognac
3 Tbsp (40mL)	olive oil
1	onion, sliced
½ tsp (5mL)	salt
	pepper
½ tsp (5mL)	thyme
1	bay leaf

Cut the rabbit into pieces and marinate for 8 to 12 hours, turning the meat frequently.

Sauté the diced pork and onions in a large saucepan until onions are transparent. Add flour, stirring to a smooth paste. Add marinade and rabbit. Combine well, then add wine and cognac. Add *bouquet garni.* Simmer, covered, for 1½ hours. Just before serving, add mushrooms and glazed onions.

Serves 4

David Gilhooly, *Sub Submarine,* 1978. Clay and glazes, 38.1 cm × 48.3 cm × 27.9 cm.

David Gilhooly

The fanciful ceramic sculptures for which David Gilhooly is famous—glazed doughnuts, Oreo cookies, chocolate puffs, ice cream sundaes, bagels oozing cream cheese and so on—are more than an extension of his mirthful personality. In a sense, they are his salvation.

"I first started to make ceramic food as a relief from eating because in the early seventies, I weighed over three hundred pounds. I found that if you made something very luscious (like the doughnut—my symbol for overweight), if you saw it, hungered for it, and yet couldn't eat it, then it would take the edge off that hunger.

"I can't remember anything really extraordinary about my childhood food. I learned to cook early and was the best student in my junior high school home economics class. It was a path to freedom for me—when I cooked, I didn't have to do dishes or go to church with my family.

"At my grandmother's, I learned to appreciate homemade noodles and smoked fish but chiefly doughnuts supplemented by trips to nearby Taco Bells and McDonald's, which I financed from the money I made playing canasta with my grandmother.

"Though I generally ate noodles and cheese and tacos as I grew up, when I could afford it I made Puerto Rican dishes learned in my childhood, many of them calling for California-grown pearl rice. I made Arroz con Pollo and a soupy version of the same thing, Asopao.

"I also stole a book from the library (ten years later I returned it) with recipes on Indian curries from an English point of view and used them. Just last year, inspired by a recipe in *Playboar*, I readjusted my rice recipes to include anything left around the house. I also heeded advice from Asian friends not to use so much water with the rice.

"But such things I principally make for company. These days I usually make myself steak, salad, and mushrooms, varying the mushrooms by frying them in butter with rice vinegar or with a teriyaki sauce.

"The most important thing for me, though, is that creating doughnuts, and Oreos, and bagels with cream cheese made it possible for me to lose eighty pounds."

Arroz con Pollo

1	large chicken, cut into pieces
2	garlic cloves, crushed
1 tsp (5mL)	oregano
2 tsp (10mL)	salt
¼ cup (50mL)	olive oil
1	green pepper, diced
1	large onion, diced
2	tomatoes, peeled, seeded and chopped
¼ cup (50mL)	sliced Spanish olives
2 Tbsp (25mL)	capers
2 cups (500mL)	rice
2½ cups (625mL)	water
1 cup (250mL)	frozen peas
1	pimento cut in strips

Wash and dry chicken pieces. Combine garlic, oregano, and salt and roll chicken in it.

Heat olive oil in a heavy frying pan. Sauté chicken until brown. Remove to a large saucepan.

Add green pepper and onion to frying pan. Sauté until soft, adding more oil if necessary. Stir in chopped tomatoes.

Transfer to saucepan with chicken pieces and add olives, capers, rice, and water. Cook, uncovered, until water is absorbed—about 20 to 25 minutes. Arrange peas and pimento strips on top. Cover and cook over low heat until rice is tender and peas are cooked—about 12 to 15 minutes.

(Note: pork, ham, or sausage may be substituted for the chicken, or a combination of chicken and sausage may be used.)

Serves 6

Basic Rice Dish

1 pound (500g)	ground beef
1	garlic clove, crushed
1	onion, finely chopped
1 tsp (5mL)	oregano
1 tsp (5mL)	salt
	freshly ground pepper
2 cups (500mL)	rice
2½ cups (625mL)	water

Brown beef in a heavy frying pan. Add garlic and onion and sauté until golden. Sprinkle with oregano, salt, and pepper. Add rice and water. Cook, uncovered, over medium heat until water is absorbed—about 20 minutes. Cover, and cook over low heat until rice is tender.

(Note: 1 pound (500g) cubed pork or 2 pounds (1kg) chicken pieces may be substituted for the beef, in which case, add ¼ cup (50mL) soy sauce to the cooking liquid.)

Serves 4

Asaro

1 pound (500g)	ground beef or pork
1	onion, finely chopped
8	boiled potatoes
2 Tbsp (25mL)	vegetable oil
1 Tbsp (15mL)	chili powder (or more to taste)
1½ tsp (7mL)	salt
	freshly ground pepper

Brown the meat in a heavy frying pan and add onion. Sauté until tender. Pour off excess fat that may have accumulated.

Mash the boiled potatoes with remaining ingredients, then combine with meat. Spoon into a greased casserole dish. Bake at 350°F (180°C) for 15 to 20 minutes to heat through.

Serve with steamed greens.

Serves 4

Cabbage Rolls

1	large cabbage
2 Tbsp (25mL)	vegetable oil
½ pound (250g)	ground beef
1	onion, finely chopped
1 tsp (5mL)	salt
2 cups (500mL)	ricotta or dry cottage cheese
1 14-ounce (398-mL)	can tomatoes

Remove outer leaves from the cabbage and cook in a large pot of boiling salted water for about 5 minutes or until they are limp. Drain and cool.

Heat oil in a heavy frying pan. Add beef and onion and sauté until meat is browned. Sprinkle with salt. Mix with ricotta or cottage cheese.

Drop a large spoonful of meat mixture on the stem end of each cabbage leaf. Roll up, tucking in ends and fasten with a toothpick. Place close together in a baking pan. Cover with tomatoes and their juice. Bake at 350°F (180°C) for 45 minutes.

Yield: about 2 dozen cabbage rolls

Torta

3 cups (750mL)	cooked and mashed zucchini
4	eggs, beaten
½ cup (125mL)	salad oil
3	garlic cloves, crushed
½ cup (125mL)	Parmesan cheese
4 slices	bread, cut in ½-inch (1-cm) cubes
1 Tbsp (15mL)	oregano
2 tsp (10mL)	salt

Mix all ingredients together. Pour into a greased 8-inch by 12-inch (3-L) pan. Bake at 350°F (180°C) for 35 to 40 minutes or until firm.

Serves 6

Pudin

1 1-pound (450-g)	loaf of white bread cut in ½-inch (1-cm) cubes
1 cup (250mL)	granulated sugar
½ cup (125mL)	brown sugar
½ cup (125mL)	melted butter
3½ tsp (20mL)	cinnamon
½ tsp (2mL)	nutmeg
½ tsp (2mL)	mace
½ tsp (2mL)	allspice
5	eggs, beaten
3 cups (750mL)	milk

Combine all ingredients and pour into a greased 10-inch by 14-inch (5-L) pan. Bake at 350°F (180°C) for 40 minutes.

Apple Cake

2	eggs
2 cups (475mL)	sugar
½ cup (125mL)	vegetable oil
4 cups (1L)	diced apple
2 cups (475mL)	flour
1 tsp (5mL)	salt
1 tsp (5mL)	nutmeg
2 tsp (10mL)	cinnamon
2 tsp (10mL)	baking soda

Beat eggs until light and frothy. Gradually add sugar and oil. Stir in diced apple.

Sift dry ingredients together. Add to eggs. Pour into greased 9-inch by 13-inch (4-L) pan. Bake at 350°F (180°C) for 1 hour. Remove from oven and cool before frosting.

Frosting

1 cup (250mL)	confectioners sugar
½ cup (125mL)	commercial sour cream
½ tsp (2mL)	baking soda

Combine all ingredients in a saucepan and stir over medium heat until mixture boils. Pour over apple cake, spreading evenly.

John Greer

When John Greer isn't in Halifax teaching at the Nova Scotia College of Art and Design, he, his wife Shirlene, and their two children live in a cozy frame house that moves with the wind on the rural south shore of Nova Scotia.

Dominating the kitchen is a huge cookstove, which is used in winter for cooking and for heating the house. In the summer, a conventional electric stove takes over. Hanging on one of the walls is an oil painting, a still life with fruit, (an early John Greer "left over from art school days"). Hanging from the huge wood beams overhead are cooking utensils: pots, pans, and popover trays all in cast iron. Kettles, ladles, racks, and skillets are all within easy reach.

Behind the century-old house is John's new studio, in front the pounding sea. In between are the vegetable patch, countless chickens, a goat, a neighbour's pig, some cattle belonging to a friend, the family dog, and numerous cats.

"We're pretty much self-sufficient," smiles John, "although we do buy such staples as avocados, artichokes, and olive oil. A local fisherman gives us scallops and we buy pickled squid, halibut, and almost anything else for around fifty cents a pound from a nearby fish plant. We eat a lot of eggs, but even so, our chickens produce more than we can use so we either trade them for other produce or give away the surplus. We get milk from our goat, and we freeze, can, dry, and otherwise preserve all the food we get from the land."

The freezer is crammed with a newly slaughtered pig. "It belonged to our neighbour, but it went mad and ran around on the loose so we had to shoot it." John got it right between the eyes with one shot. Local superstition said it was wild because of being inbred and the neighbours all said it would be inedible, but "actually, it's just fine and we're really enjoying it."

The Greers recently made turtle soup. It may have been for the first and last time. "We saw this snapping turtle on the road so we brought it home in the back of the truck. It took over half an hour to coax it to stick its head out so we could chop it off. Finally it did, and so we did!" laughs John. "We worked at putting the soup together according to endless pages of directions in a cookbook, and in the end we didn't like it all that much. The broth was very strong and the meat tough and rubbery. Never again."

Cheese Bread

1 tsp (5mL)	sugar
½ cup (125mL)	lukewarm water
1 package	yeast
2 cups (475mL)	hot milk or hot vegetable water
3 Tbsp (40mL)	sugar or 1½ Tbsp (25mL) honey
1 Tbsp (15mL)	salt
1½ Tbsp (25mL)	salad oil
¼ tsp (1mL)	oregano
¼ tsp (1mL)	basil
¼ tsp (1mL)	powdered garlic
4½ to 5 cups (1L)	flour (unbleached or a mixture of white and whole wheat)
1	onion, finely diced
1 cup (250mL)	grated cheese (Cheddar or Parmesan or a mixture of hard cheeses)

In a small bowl, dissolve sugar in water. Sprinkle in yeast. Set aside for 10 minutes.

In a large bowl stir together the hot milk, sugar, salt, oil, and herbs. Cool until lukewarm. Add the yeast mixture. Stir in 2 cups (500mL) of the flour and beat well until smooth. Add the onion and grated cheese. Continue adding flour until the dough becomes too stiff to stir, then turn out onto a floured board and knead until smooth and elastic, adding more flour as necessary to produce a firm, non-sticky dough.

Shape dough into a ball and place in a large buttered bowl, turning dough so all sides are buttered. Cover with a towel and set to rise in a warm draft-free place until double in bulk—about 1½ hours.

Grease a 2½-quart (2.5-L) casserole or soufflé dish.

Punch dough down and knead on board for 2 to 3 minutes. Shape into a ball and place in prepared casserole dish. Cover with a towel and set to rise until at least 1 inch (2.5cm) above the rim of the dish.

Bake at 350°F (180°C) for about 45 minutes. Remove to a rack to cool before slicing.

Popovers

1 cup (250mL)	flour
¼ tsp (1mL)	salt
2	eggs
1 cup (250mL)	milk
1 Tbsp (15mL)	melted shortening

Sift together the flour and salt. In a separate bowl, beat eggs. Add milk and shortening, then gradually stir in the flour mixture. Beat with a rotary beater until smooth. Let stand for 30 minutes.

Grease 8 custard cups or iron muffin tins well. Preheat in a 450°F (230°C) oven for 10 minutes.

Fill cups half full with batter. Bake at 450°F (230°C) for 20 minutes. Reduce heat to 350°F (180°C) and bake for a further 15 minutes. Serve hot.

Yield: 8 popovers

Solomon Gundy

6	salt herring
3 cups (750mL)	vinegar
¾ cup (175mL)	sugar
3	onions, thinly sliced
1 tsp (5mL)	dried dill or a few sprigs of fresh dill
4	bay leaves
1 tsp (5mL)	bruised whole allspice

Fillet salt herring. Remove or retain skin as desired. Soak overnight in cold water.

Bring remaining ingredients to a boil. Reduce heat and simmer for 20 minutes.

Rinse herring fillets in several changes of cold water, then put them in a small crock. Cover the fish with the hot vinegar mixture. Cover and refrigerate for at least 6 days.

Serve with fresh onion, dill or sour cream.

John Greer, *A Little Taste (Spoon Fed Culture)* (detail), 1977. Photograph, 16.3 cm × 18.6 cm.

Housebankin'

1 pound (500g)	salt cod
2 pounds (1kg)	potatoes (approx. 6 medium)
¼ cup (50mL)	milk
2 Tbsp (25mL)	butter
	salt and pepper
½ pound (250g)	salt pork, finely diced
2	onions, finely diced
1 Tbsp (15mL)	cider vinegar
1 Tbsp (15mL)	brown sugar
3 Tbsp (40mL)	butter
1 cup (250mL)	cream

Place salt cod in a saucepan. Cover with water. Bring to the boil and drain off water. Repeat process, drain, and set cod aside.

Boil potatoes until soft. Drain and mash with milk and butter. Combine with fish and season with salt and pepper. Set aside.

Fry diced salt pork in a heavy frying pan until crisp. Add onion and sauté until golden. Add cider vinegar, brown sugar, butter, and cream.

Grease a 2½-quart (2.5-L) casserole dish and fill with the potato and fish mixture. Cover with salt pork and onion sauce. Bake at 350°F (180°C) for 20 minutes, or until heated through.

Serve with mustard pickles.

Serves 4

Scrapple

1	pig head
2	stalks celery
1	onion, diced
1 Tbsp (15mL)	salt
6	peppercorns
4 cups (1L)	cornmeal
2	onions, finely chopped
3 tsp (15mL)	salt
3 tsp (15mL)	pepper
2 tsp (10mL)	sage
2 tsp (10mL)	thyme

Scald the hair off the pig head. Discard the eyes and ears. Brush the teeth with a stiff bristle brush. Cut the head into quarters or eighths (depending on size) or have the butcher do this.

Simmer head, brain, and tongue in about 4 quarts (4L) of water to which the celery, onion, salt, and peppercorns have been added, for 4 hours. Remove any scum that may form on the surface.

Strain off the stock and reserve. Measure it and either boil to reduce or add more water to make 3 quarts (3L).

Remove meat from the bones and reserve. Discard bones and some of the fat.

Bring the stock to a boil. Slowly add cornmeal or a mixture of cornmeal and oatmeal. Cook until it forms a thick mash, stirring constantly, for about 20 minutes, then add reserved meat, chopped onions, salt, pepper, sage, and thyme. Cover and cook over low heat for 10 to 15 minutes. Pour into 4 loaf pans. Chill until firm.

To serve, slice and eat cold or slice and fry in fat in a hot frying pan.

Yield: 4 loaves

Jerry Grey

In the past, Ottawa painter Jerry Grey used to cook foods that took hours to prepare—often for entertaining as many as fifty friends at once—but now she prefers to spend as little time as is necessary standing in the kitchen.

"It is amazing how you can get by with less fancy things as long as you have great big bowls of salted nuts for people to eat," she laughs.

"Even though I cook less than before, I still plan my menus according to the colour, texture, and flavour of the foods. I know, for instance, that potatoes are too slimy to accompany black Alaska cod and that brown rice cuts its saltiness, so I'll use rice when I'm poaching cod. I also like the balance of texture and colour between beans and mushrooms—I often combine them.

"I invent my way through something and usually I know when I 'get it,' " she says. "I'm building something when I cook and I keep in mind what the various flavours are as I go along.

"I love fish and seafood so I cook them a lot. They're relatively quick to do, too. I also adore salads. I could spend hours on salads. I make them up as I go along, too, often combining unlikely ingredients like radishes and apples. For dressings I may mix mayonnaise or yoghurt with lemon juice because I don't like a sweet dressing."

What is the most important cooking ingredient for Jerry Grey? "Garlic. I love garlic. I have to have it. Cooking without garlic is a disaster," she says.

Photo: Jerry Grey and David Knowles

Jerry Grey's Cold Green Meat Loaf

1½ pounds (750g)	ground veal
1 pound (500g)	ground pork
2	eggs
½ cup (125mL)	fine dry bread crumbs
¾ cup (175mL)	chopped fresh parsley
½ cup (125mL)	chopped chives
1 cup (250mL)	chopped fresh basil leaves, or ⅓ cup (75mL) dried basil
¼ cup (50mL)	chopped green pepper
1 tsp (5mL)	dry mustard
1 tsp (5mL)	salt
	freshly ground pepper
1 tsp (5mL)	Worcestershire sauce
3 dashes of	Tabasco sauce
	bacon strips
2	lemons, finely sliced

Combine all ingredients except bacon and lemon slices.

Line a 2-quart (2-L) pâté mold with bacon strips. Pack in the ground meat mixture. Lay lemon slices on top and enclose with ends of bacon strips. Cover lightly with aluminum foil. Bake at 350°F (180°C) for 1½ hours. Drain off bacon fat and chill, weighing loaf down with heavy cans or a brick.

To serve, unmold and cut in ½-inch (1-cm) slices. Nice when accompanied by a Greek salad.

Spinach and Eggplant Soufflé

3	medium eggplants
½ cup (125mL)	butter
1 cup (250mL)	flour
1 tsp (5mL)	salt
2 cups (500mL)	milk
8	egg yolks, beaten
1 cup (250mL)	chopped fresh spinach
2 tsp (10mL)	dry mustard
pinch of	cayenne
pinch of	pepper
1 cup (250mL)	grated Cheddar cheese
½ cup (125mL)	grated Parmesan cheese
1 Tbsp (15mL)	chopped parsley
10	egg whites
½ tsp (2mL)	cream of tartar

Cut eggplants in half lengthwise. Place cut side down in a roasting pan. Add enough boiling water to reach half an inch (2cm) up the sides of the eggplant halves. Bake at 350°F (180°C) for 30 minutes or until pulp is tender. Cool. Scrape out pulp leaving ¼ inch (5mm) in the shell. Discard pulp.

Butter a 3-quart (3-L) soufflé dish well. Tie a double layer of waxed paper around the upper edge of the dish to form a collar. Line with eggplant shells, purple side out.

Melt butter. Stir in flour and salt. Gradually add milk. Stir until thickened. Remove from heat. Stir a large spoonful into beaten egg yolks, then pour all back into saucepan. Combine thoroughly. Add remaining ingredients except egg whites and cream of tartar and set aside to cool to room temperature.

Beat egg whites and cream of tartar until stiff. Fold into egg yolk mixture. Gently pour into prepared soufflé dish. Bake at 350°F (180°C) for 80 minutes or until firm.

To serve, invert on a large heated platter. Garnish with watercress and cherry tomatoes.
Serves 8 to 10

Cauliflower Elegant

	Marinade
½ cup (125mL)	olive oil
	juice of half a lemon
3 Tbsp (40mL)	cider or wine vinegar
1 tsp (5mL)	salt
¼ tsp (1mL)	sugar
¼ tsp (1mL)	pepper
	Vegetables
1	raw cauliflower, cut into florets and thinly sliced
½	red onion, finely diced
1 Tbsp (15mL)	chopped parsley
1 cup (250mL)	strips of green pepper
1 7-ounce (200-mL)	jar pimento, finely sliced
1 14-ounce (398-mL)	can ripe olives, drained and sliced

Prepare marinade by combining ingredients. Toss with vegetables. Refrigerate, covered, for several hours before serving. Drain off excess liquid and serve vegetables on Bibb lettuce leaves or in an elegant glass bowl.

Serves 8

Previous page:
Ted Harrison, *The Stove Fires are Burning,* 1981.
Acrylic, 30.5 cm × 23 cm. Collection of the artist.
Photo: Mladen P. Kasalica.

Ted Harrison

"It's a bit hard for me to discuss food with any great passion right at this instant because I'm on a diet," says Yukon artist Ted Harrison. "But in all honesty, I care a lot about food."

As an art student in England, Ted spent a summer as an assistant cook in a hotel in the seaside town of Scarborough. "The Royal Hotel where I worked in the pâtisserie kitchen was owned by Charles Laughton's brother. Every morning I got up at five o'clock and baked three hundred buns. Then I did trifles and *rhum babas* and all sorts of other delicious sweets."

The Harrisons have lived all over the world, so they have a very international approach to food. And even though they have lived in Whitehorse for the past nine years, Ted says he can pretty well always obtain most of the ingredients he needs to cook the interesting foods they like.

"We have fine supermarkets and an excellent delicatessen here," he says, "and also many great restaurants. So I can make my Mexican and Chinese recipes and even occasionally get things like smoked eels which we used to love eating in New Zealand. Besides, if I can't get something I need, I'll make up other ingredients.

"There are four of us in our house: my wife Nicky, my son Charles, our dog Brunhilde, and myself. Brunhilde tends to turn up her nose at human food, although I have not yet tried her on haggis. I should do that, perhaps. The rest of us all like it."

Moose Stew

4 pounds (2kg)	moose meat
4	carrots, sliced
3	medium onions, diced
3	medium potatoes, diced
½ cup (125mL)	dried barley
1 tsp (5mL)	garlic salt
¼ tsp (1mL)	pepper
3 cups (750mL)	cold water
½ cup (125mL)	butter
1 tsp (5mL)	meat extract
1 Tbsp (15mL)	Yorkshire relish
¾ cup (175mL)	sherry

Put meat, vegetables and barley in an earthenware crock pot. Add garlic salt, pepper, and water. Bring to the boil. Stir in remaining ingredients.

Cover, reduce heat, and simmer slowly for 3 hours, stirring occasionally. Add more water if necessary.

Serves 8

Trifle à l'Anglais

1 9-inch (23-cm)	round sponge cake
1	package Jello
1 cup (250mL)	boiling water
1 14-ounce (398-mL)	can fruit cocktail, drained
½ cup (125mL)	sherry
4 Tbsp (50mL)	custard powder
3 Tbsp (30mL)	sugar
2½ cups (625mL)	warm milk
1 cup (250mL)	whipping cream

Place the sponge cake in the bottom of a deep bowl. Prepare the Jello using the cup of boiling water. Stir in the drained fruit cocktail and the sherry and pour over the sponge cake. Set aside in a cool place until Jello is firm.

Combine custard powder and sugar in a saucepan. Gradually stir in milk. Stir over medium heat until thickened, then pour over fruit mixture. Chill.

Just before serving, whip the cream and spread over custard layer. Garnish with cherries, nuts, or anything of your choice.

Serves 8

Gershon Iskowitz

"When you're cooking, there are so many things you have to be conscious of," says Gershon Iskowitz. "Appearance, colour, and texture, for instance. And people's tastes. Like when you're using garlic, perhaps you want to put in several cloves because you really like it, but you have to be considerate of other people who are also going to be eating it."

Somewhere in the jumble of Gershon Iskowitz's walk-up apartment-cum-painter's studio in Toronto is the kitchen that is the scene of many fabulous meals. His fellow artists across Canada are quick to praise his prowess in the kitchen and he loves to entertain them whenever they visit Toronto. A favourite seems to be his Hearty Chicken Borscht.

"Well, it's a good example of how you have to add ingredients at precisely the right time in order for it to come out right. You have to stand over the pot for hours, tasting it every few minutes to make sure.

"I remember my mother could make something from nothing, spending all afternoon tasting whatever it was she was cooking to bring it to perfection. I do the same thing. But I also like to eat out!"

Hearty Chicken Borscht

2	marrow bones
3 quarts (3L)	water
4 pounds (2kg)	chicken, skinned and cut into serving pieces
3	garlic cloves, crushed
1	small red cabbage, shredded
2	carrots, peeled and thinly sliced
2	potatoes, peeled and thinly sliced
2	tomatoes, peeled, seeded, and chopped
½ pound (250g)	mushrooms, thinly sliced
1	small cauliflower, broken into clusters of florets
3	cooked beets, thinly sliced and their cooking liquid
1	onion, diced
1 Tbsp (15mL)	vegetable oil
	salt and pepper
	juice of 1 lemon
1 Tbsp (15mL)	honey

Boil marrow bones and water in a large saucepan for 30 minutes. Remove bones and discard. Add chicken pieces, crushed garlic, and shredded cabbage to the liquid. Simmer, covered, for 20 minutes. Add carrots and potatoes and simmer for 10 minutes. Then add tomatoes, mushrooms, cauliflower, and beets with their liquid. Add diced onion which has been sautéed in vegetable oil until golden. Cover and simmer for a further 10 minutes. Add salt and pepper to taste. Add lemon juice and honey.

Serve in large open soup bowls accompanied by black rye bread and unsalted butter.

Serves 8 to 10

Hamburgers

1½ pounds (750g)	ground beef
2	garlic cloves, crushed
	salt and pepper
2 slices	white bread
1	egg
¼ cup (50mL)	vegetable oil

Place ground beef on a cutting board. Season with crushed garlic. Sprinkle with salt and pepper. Dip bread slices in water and wring out. Put bread and egg on top of meat. With a cleaver or butcher knife, chop all ingredients together to mix well.

Heat vegetable oil in a heavy frying pan. With wet hands, form meat into 6 patties ½ inch (1cm) thick. Fry 5 minutes per side in hot oil, for medium hamburgers. Adjust time for rare or well done.

Serve with mashed potatoes and a shot of vodka.

Serves 6

Chicken Burgers

2 cups (500mL)	ground raw chicken meat
2	garlic cloves, crushed
	salt and pepper
2 slices	white bread
1	egg
¼ cup (50mL)	vegetable oil

Place chicken on a cutting board. Season with crushed garlic. Sprinkle with salt and pepper. Dip bread slices in water and wring out. Put bread and egg on top of meat. With a cleaver or butcher knife, chop all ingredients together to mix well.

Heat vegetable oil in a heavy frying pan. With wet hands, form meat into 6 patties ½ inch (1cm) thick. Fry 10 minutes per side in hot oil.

Serves 6

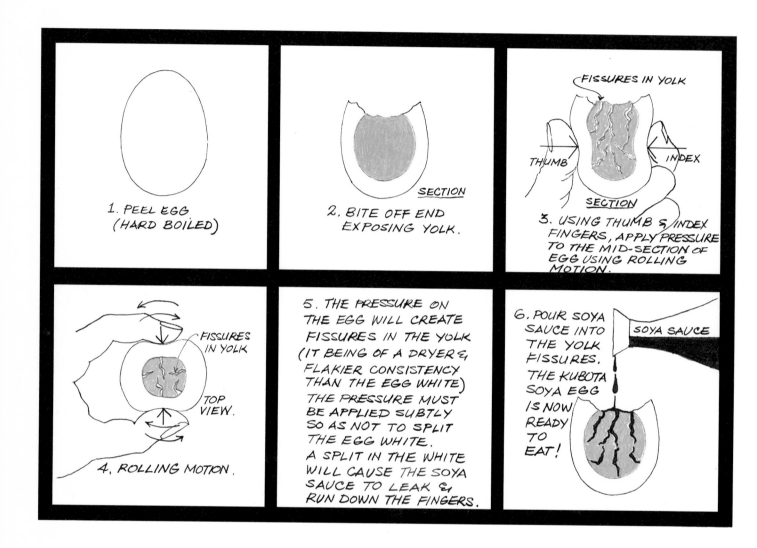

Nobuo Kubota, *Kubota Soya Egg,* 1979. Pencil and
pen, series, each 10.3 cm × 10.2 cm. Photo: Mladen P.
Kasalica.

Nobuo Kubota

The Kubota family enjoys its food with an enthusiasm that is infectious. Nobuo and Lee talk about it in a manner that borders on the lyrical—"Our Jessica is a bacon freak of rare commitment"—and they are celebrated among their friends in Toronto for having a repertoire of unusual and entertaining dishes.

Their beef, pork, and shrimp fondue with tempura is an example. "When we entertain with this meal, the entire evening centres around the table. It goes on for hours at a leisurely pace, with sake, wine, and champagne in between forays to the fondue pots. This is a marvellous effort, worth all the trouble of preparation."

Or consider the Famous Kubota Soya Egg for which Nobuo and Lee give the following directions:

"Bite off the top of a hard-boiled egg until part of the egg yolk is exposed. Holding the bitten side up, gently roll and squeeze the egg between the fingers till little cracks form in the yolk. A delicate touch is necessary so that you don't inadvertently split the white of the egg, thereby dooming it to the egg-salad bowl. Now carefully pour a few drops of soy sauce into the yolk while you again work it around with your fingers, so that the soy sauce travels down through the cracks in the yolk. Then nibble away politely or just shove the whole delicious mess into your mouth at once and pig it down."

As Lee adds, "These little treasures are great picnic fare. With conscientious practice, you'll become so adept at working the yolk that you'll

never have to walk around with soy sauce spots on your T-shirt.

"Nobby is considering approaching David Suzuki about co-teaching a credit course with him next year. Nobby would teach egg manipulation and David could teach chopstick aptitude from a genetic point of view."

Breakfast Soup

4 Tbsp (50mL)	cooked cold brown rice
1 Tbsp (15mL)	miso (soybean paste available in Oriental food stores)
1 cup (250mL)	chicken stock
1	egg (broken into a small dish) any or all of the following vegetables: thin strips of carrot, turnip, celery, green beans, shredded spinach, cauliflower florets or broccoli florets
1	green onion, shredded dried seaweed and dried fish flakes (optional) soy sauce (optional)

Place rice and miso in a large individual soup bowl.

Bring stock to a boil in a saucepan and pour a couple of spoonfuls of it into soup bowl to break up the miso. Return saucepan to heat and bring again to the boil. Carefully lower egg into stock, reduce heat and simmer, covered, for 1 minute. Add a spoonful of each of the vegetables, cover, and simmer for another minute or until egg is poached. With a slotted spoon, lift egg from the stock. Pour stock into soup bowl containing rice and miso; then, top with the egg. Sprinkle with seaweed, fish flakes, and soy sauce if desired.

Serves 1

Wiener Fried Rice

2 Tbsp (25mL)	peanut oil
2	raw wieners, each cut diagonally into 6 pieces
1	small onion, finely chopped
4 cups (1L)	cooked rice
½ cup (125mL)	cooked peas
1 Tbsp (15mL)	soy sauce salt and pepper

Heat oil in wok and brown wiener pieces over medium heat. Remove and keep warm. Sauté onion in oil until golden, then add rice. Stir until lightly browned and heated through. Add wieners, peas, and soy sauce. Add salt and pepper to taste.

(Note: Bacon Fried Rice may be made using several strips of bacon cut up and fried instead of the wieners. Pour off all but 2 tablespoons (25mL) bacon fat and proceed as for Wiener Fried Rice.)

Serves 2 or 3

Rice Balls

a bowl of	vinegar and water
4 cups (1L)	cold cooked Japanese rice
2 dozen	salted pickled plums (available in Oriental food stores)
1 cup (250mL)	toasted sesame seeds

Moisten hands by dipping in bowl of vinegar and water. Take about ¼ cup (50mL) rice in one hand. Make an indentation in it and stuff a pickled plum in the hollow. Press rice around plum to cover completely, forming a ball about the size of a small apple. Roll in sesame seeds and set aside on a plate. Continue until all rice is used. Refrigerate.

Yield: 2 dozen balls

Beef and Pork Fondue with Shrimp and Vegetable Tempura

Meat and Fish

1½ pounds (750g)	beef tenderloin, cut in 1-inch (2.5-cm) cubes
1½ pounds (750g)	pork tenderloin, cut in 1-inch (2.5-cm) cubes
2 pounds (1kg)	raw shrimp, shelled and deveined

Vegetables

1	cauliflower, broken into florets
1 bunch	broccoli, broken into florets
2	green peppers, cut in bite-sized chunks
2	red peppers, cut in bite-sized chunks
½ pound (250g)	mushroom caps, wiped clean
2	onions, cut in rings
1 pound (500g)	green beans, ends removed
1	sweet potato, cut in finger shapes and parboiled for 5 minutes
1	white potato, cut in finger shapes and parboiled for 5 minutes
3	zucchini, cut in ½-inch (1-cm) slices

Sauce 1

1 cup (250mL)	*dashi* (chicken stock)
½ cup (125mL)	light soy sauce
½ cup (125mL)	dark soy sauce
1 tsp (5mL)	sesame seed oil
½ cup (125mL)	ground sesame seeds
½ tsp (2mL)	finely chopped chili pepper
1 Tbsp (15mL)	rice vinegar
½ tsp (2mL)	hot green horseradish (available canned in Japanese markets)
1 Tbsp (15mL)	lemon juice

Combine all sauce ingredients. Bring to a boil, then set aside to cool.

Sauce 2

1 cup (250mL)	*dashi* (chicken stock)
⅓ cup (75mL)	*mirin* (flavoured sake)
⅓ cup (75mL)	light soy sauce
1 Tbsp (15mL)	finely grated daikon (similar to horseradish, available fresh at Japanese markets)

Combine all ingredients. Bring to a boil, then set aside to cool.

Sauce 3

½ cup (125mL)	soy sauce
½ cup (125mL)	*mirin* (flavoured sake)
1 Tbsp (15mL)	lemon juice
1 Tbsp (15mL)	finely grated fresh ginger root

Combine all ingredients. Bring to a boil, then set aside to cool.

Tempura Batter (for shrimp and vegetables)

1 cup (250mL)	flour
3 Tbsp (40mL)	peanut oil
¾ cup (175mL)	lukewarm water
1	egg white beaten until stiff

Just before serving, mix flour, oil and lukewarm water together. Then fold in egg white.

To make and serve at the table:

Set up 2 or 3 fondue pots filled with hot peanut oil and provide 2 fondue forks or sticks per guest. The dishes of meats, shrimp, vegetables, and sauces should be placed on the table within reach of all.

Guests may spear 2 or 3 pieces of meat and cook them in the hot oil. Or they may dip the shrimp and vegetables in the batter and cook them in the hot oil. The cooked food is then dipped in the sauces. Make more tempura batter if needed.

Serves 8

Suzy Lake

Suzy Lake, who recently moved to Toronto from Montreal with her husband Alex Neumann, loves her new neighbourhood. "There is a super ethnic mix around here so we have access to all sorts of interesting foods. The variety of things that we can get at Kensington Market is unbelievable, and just a short distance away is the Knob Hill Farm's Food Terminal—the most immense supermarket imaginable."

It was only a few years ago when she went to Europe that Suzy had her eyes and taste buds exposed to fine food for the first time. "I grew up with a mother who was a good but plain cook so I was never exposed to 'different' foods. Can you believe that it wasn't until I went to Europe that I discovered such delights as herring?"

Today, things are different. Suzy cooks from a variety of international cuisines and enjoys experimenting in the kitchen when she can find the time between her art, her photography, and her teaching position at the University of Guelph. Alex's Hungarian aunt has shared some favourite traditional recipes with her and she likes to do Swiss fondue and several German dishes.

"I cook pretty much with my hands," says Suzy. "And I'm a 'some' cook—some of this and some of that."

She also cooks with an eye to economy, working wonders with cheaper cuts of meat. Short ribs or cross ribs dressed up with a barbecue sauce make a good company dish and Suzy makes them frequently because they're Alex's favourite. She also does a lot of roasts because of their stretching qualities. One day's roast becomes the next day's meat pie, and the remaining bones get simmered into a soup. "Nothing is wasted around here," says Suzy.

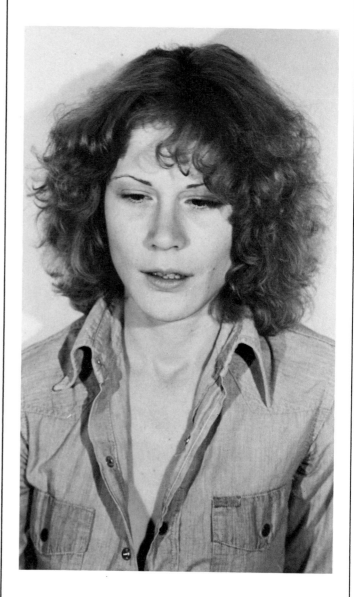

Chicken Paprika

4 pounds (2kg)	chicken
¼ cup (50mL)	chicken fat
1	onion, finely chopped
2	garlic cloves, crushed
2 Tbsp (25mL)	Hungarian sweet paprika
1 tsp (5mL)	salt
	water
2 cups (500mL)	commercial sour cream

Wash chicken, cut into serving pieces and dry thoroughly.

Heat chicken fat in a heavy frying pan. Sauté chopped onion until soft. Add garlic and chicken pieces and cook, turning, until golden brown on all sides. Add sweet paprika, salt, and enough water to cover. Cover and simmer for 1 hour.

Just before serving, remove chicken to a heated platter and keep warm. Add sour cream to the sauce remaining in the frying pan. Combine thoroughly. Heat through but do not allow to boil.

Serve chicken on a bed of noodles or accompanied by gnocchi. Spoon sauce over the chicken and noodles and sprinkle with chopped parsley.

Serves 4

Pea Soup

12 cups (3L)	water
1	ham bone
1 pound (500g)	dried split green peas
2	onions, chopped
2 tsp (10mL)	garlic powder
2 tsp (10mL)	tarragon
2 Tbsp (25mL)	chopped parsley

Pour water into a large saucepan. Add ham bone and split green peas. Cover and let stand overnight.

Add remaining ingredients and bring to the boil. Reduce heat and simmer, covered, for 3 hours.

Serves 16

Cross Ribs with Barbecue Sauce

1 cup (250mL)	tomato ketchup
¼ cup (50mL)	soy sauce
2 Tbsp (25mL)	brown sugar
½ cup (125mL)	finely chopped onion
6 or 7 pounds (3kg)	cross ribs

Combine the ketchup, soy sauce, brown sugar, and chopped onion into a smooth sauce.

Place cross ribs in a shallow baking pan. Brush well with sauce. Bake at 350°F (180°C) for 45 minutes, basting occasionally with sauce.

Serves 6

German Potato Salad

3	large potatoes
3	hard-boiled eggs
¼ pound (125g)	bacon, diced
¼ cup (50mL)	diced celery
2 Tbsp (25mL)	sliced radishes
2 Tbsp (25mL)	chopped onion
2 Tbsp (25mL)	diced green pepper
1 Tbsp (15mL)	vinegar
1 tsp (5mL)	brown sugar
½ tsp (2mL)	garlic powder
1 tsp (5mL)	salt
	freshly ground pepper
2 Tbsp (25mL)	chopped parsley

Boil potatoes in salted water until tender. Drain well and cut into ½-inch (1-cm) cubes. Remove shells and coarsely chop hard-boiled eggs. Add to potatoes and set aside.

Cook bacon in a heavy frying pan until crisp. Remove with a slotted spoon and set aside. Pour off all fat except for 3 tablespoons (40mL). Add celery, radishes, onion, and green pepper. Sauté for 3 minutes. Return bacon to pan and add vinegar, sugar, seasonings and parsley. Combine thoroughly. Stir in potatoes and hard-boiled eggs. Toss until heated through.

Serve hot or cold.

Serves 6

Braised European Blade Roast

1 Tbsp (15mL)	vegetable oil
1	onion, cut in rings
1 3-pound (1.5-kg)	blade roast
	salt and pepper
2 tsp (10mL)	dry mustard

Heat oil in a heavy frying pan and sauté onion rings until browned. Place in bottom of a shallow baking pan.

Sprinkle roast with salt and pepper and rub with mustard. Place it on top of the onions.

Set shallow pan in a large roasting pan into which has been poured half an inch (1cm) of water. Cover and cook at 325°F (160°C) for 2 hours. Uncover and cook for a further 30 minutes.

Serves 6

Suzy's Egg Nog

4 cups (1L)	milk
1 cup (250mL)	sugar
4	eggs
	freshly grated nutmeg
1 cup (250mL)	brandy

Combine all ingredients in a blender.

Mix together on a low speed for 30 seconds.

Heat in a large saucepan over medium heat, stirring constantly, until mixture thickens. Blend briefly in blender. Chill thoroughly before serving.

Yield: 1½ quarts (1.5L)

Rita Letendre and Kosso Eloul

"There are more cookbooks in this house than there are art books," says sculptor Kosso Eloul, who lives with his wife, painter Rita Letendre, and their faithful, affectionate Doberman Pinscher, Yaffa, in a large red-brick house in downtown Toronto. The house is filled with sunlight, sculptures, paintings, and lush plants.

Big as the house is, people seem to congregate in the kitchen. Rita designed it to have everything at hand and within easy reach without "having to rummage around and rearrange everything to get what I want." The counters were built to suit her diminutive height. A large work table with its chopping-block top dominates the room. It has a trap door in it for scraping the garbage through, and open shelves below for storage. Above it hang pots and pans. The floor is covered in earth-toned tiles. The walls are lined with racks holding clear jars filled with grains, pastas, and beans, and behind louvred doors is tucked a well-stocked spice cabinet.

Rita understands the subtleties of spices and has an affinity for them. She experiments with "a little of this and a little of that," often trying a recipe five or six times until she gets what she's looking for. She also likes the tang that frozen orange juice concentrate gives a recipe, and uses it frequently with spectacular results.

There is almost no limit to the lengths that Rita will go to, to acquire ingredients. "Some years ago, we were on our way to Mexico, and we stopped off in San Francisco, where a woman gave me some sourdough starter whose original culture was over a hundred years old, having come from the supplies of a gold-rush family.

"I had the starter in a jar, wrapped in plastic, and I carried it everywhere with me for over a month. On airplanes and in hotels I'd ask to have it refrigerated, and I kept a little tag on my purse to remind me of it."

Kosso and Rita appreciate all cuisines, both for their own enjoyment and for entertaining, but, as Kosso says, "I really like Middle Eastern and Oriental foods best because they're made up of little tastes of so many things. It's the first sensation that's exciting. The rest is just stuffing to achieve a full feeling."

Cornish Hens with Bulghur

3 Tbsp	(40mL)	orange juice concentrate
3 Tbsp	(40mL)	grated lemon peel
2 Tbsp	(25mL)	vegetable oil
1 tsp	(5mL)	ground coriander
½ tsp	(2mL)	freshly ground pepper
¼ tsp	(1mL)	thyme
4		Cornish hens
4 Tbsp	(50mL)	melted butter
4 Tbsp	(50mL)	honey

Bulghur

3 Tbsp	(40mL)	butter
2		celery stalks with tops, chopped
1		large onion, finely chopped
1 Tbsp	(15mL)	fennel seed
1 Tbsp	(15mL)	allspice
1 Tbsp	(15mL)	zhartar
1		crushed cardamom seed
1½ cup	(375mL)	coarse bulghur
¾ cup	(175mL)	chicken stock
½ cup	(125mL)	roasted pine nuts
1 cup	(250mL)	dark raisins
1 Tbsp	(15mL)	rose water

Combine orange juice concentrate, lemon peel, oil, coriander, pepper, and thyme. Set aside.

Wash the hens thoroughly and pat dry with paper towels. Brush inside and out with the orange marinade, and truss. Set in a shallow baking pan. Let stand for 2 hours.

Pour melted butter over hens. Bake at 475°F (240°C) for 12 to 15 minutes or until brown. Reduce heat to 375°F (190°C) and cook for 45 minutes. Lower heat to 275°F (140°C) and cook for 15 minutes during which time the hens should be basted with the pan juices to which 4 tablespoons (50mL) honey are added.

To prepare bulghur, melt butter in a heavy frying pan set over low heat. Add celery, onion, fennel, allspice, zhartar, and cardamom, and cook, stirring for 5 minutes. Add bulghur and chicken stock, stirring to combine. Cover and simmer until tender—about 15 to 20 minutes. Stir in pine nuts and raisins and cook, uncovered, until all liquid has evaporated. Add rose water.

Mound bulghur in the centre of a heated platter. Surround with Cornish hens. Decorate with parsley and orange slices.

Serves 4

Yoghurt Soup

3 Tbsp	(40mL)	butter
3 Tbsp	(40mL)	flour
4 cups	(1L)	chicken stock
1 cup	(250mL)	natural yoghurt
1½ Tbsp	(25mL)	dried mint
1 tsp	(5mL)	paprika
		butter
		paprika
4		mint leaves

Melt butter in a large saucepan. Stir in flour. Gradually add half the chicken stock, stirring constantly until mixture thickens.

In another bowl, combine the yoghurt with remaining stock. Add to the saucepan along with the dried mint and 1 teaspoon (5mL) paprika. Heat through but do not allow to boil.

Serve in heated soup bowls. Top with a dab of butter, a sprinkling of paprika, and a fresh mint leaf.

Serves 4

Pear Preserve

24		small bosc pears, stems intact
3 cups	(750mL)	sugar
4 cups	(1L)	water
½		cinnamon stick
2		cloves
4		cardamom seeds, broken
1		lemon, cut in pieces
		brandy

Wash pears. Combine remaining ingredients except brandy in a large saucepan. Bring to a boil and simmer, covered, for 5 minutes. Add pears and continue to simmer until tender but still firm—about 10 to 15 minutes.

Spoon pears into sterile wide-mouth sealer jars. Pour in syrup and spices to ¾ full. Fill to the brim with brandy. Seal jars tightly.

Store in a cool dark place for 3 months before serving, shaking occasionally.

Yield: 5 quarts (5L)

Fruit Compote

1	large orange
2	large apples
3	peaches
6	pears
1	lemon
2 cups (500mL)	sugar
½ cup (125mL)	water
3	whole cardamom seeds

Peel the orange, discarding the rind, and cut pulp into ½-inch (1-cm) pieces. Discard core from the apples and chop. Remove skin from peaches and pears and cut in small pieces. Chop lemon very fine, including the rind.

Combine sugar, water, and cardamom seeds in a medium saucepan. Bring to the boil. Add fruits, reduce heat, and simmer, covered, for 1 hour.

Serve warm or cold.

Serves 8

Honey Cakes

2 cups (475mL)	olive oil, heated
2 pounds (1kg)	fine wheat semolina
⅓ cup (75mL)	granulated sugar
2 Tbsp (25mL)	water
	juice and rind of 1 orange
3 Tbsp (40mL)	frozen orange juice concentrate
½ tsp (2mL)	cinnamon
¼ tsp (1mL)	ground cloves
2 tsp (10mL)	baking powder
½ cup (125mL)	cherry brandy

Syrup

1 cup (250mL)	sugar
1 cup (250mL)	liquid honey
1½ cups (375mL)	water
½ cup (125mL)	rose water

Pour hot olive oil over semolina. Stir well, then add remaining cake ingredients, combining thoroughly.

Knead together, then form into small cakes the size and shape of an egg. Place on a greased baking pan. Bake at 350°F (180°C) for 35 minutes.

While cakes are baking, make syrup by boiling all ingredients together for 5 minutes in a wide shallow saucepan or frying pan. Add hot cooked honey cakes and simmer for 5 minutes, spooning the syrup over them so that it is all absorbed. Drain on a wire rack.

Yield: 4 dozen honey cakes

Sourdough Bread

1 cup (250mL)	sourdough starter
2 cups (500mL)	milk
2 cups (500mL)	unbleached white flour
1 Tbsp (15mL)	sugar
1 cup (250mL)	soy granules, soaked in a bowl of lukewarm water to cover
1 cup (250mL)	bulghur, soaked in a bowl of lukewarm water to cover
½ cup (125mL)	vegetable oil
1 Tbsp (15mL)	salt
5 cups (1.25L)	unbleached flour (approx.)

In a large bowl, combine sourdough starter, milk, 2 cups (500mL) flour, and sugar. Leave overnight in a warm place. Soak soy granules and bulghur overnight.

The next day, remove 1 cup (250mL) of the starter/flour mixture and use to replenish starter supply. Add oil and salt to remaining dough. Drain water off soy granules and bulghur and mix with dough.

Gradually add flour, beating with a spoon until too stiff to mix, then turn out onto a floured board and knead, incorporating enough remaining flour to form a stiff dough. Knead until smooth and elastic—about 5 to 10 minutes.

Shape dough into a ball and place in a large buttered bowl, turning dough so all sides are buttered. Cover with a towel and set to rise in a warm, draft-free place until double in bulk—about 1½ hours.

Punch dough down and turn out onto a floured board. Divide into 3 balls and knead each for 2 to 3 minutes. Shape into 3 long loaves. Place on greased baking pans, cover with a towel and set to rise in a warm place for 1 to 2 hours. Bake at 375°F (190°C) for 50 minutes.

Yield: 3 sourdough loaves

Grant Macdonald

Grant Macdonald's bright, airy Kingston home sits on the edge of Lake Ontario. Grant lives there alone painting in his large studio and looking forward to opportunities to cook for friends. His kitchen is small, but it is the scene of much activity.

"I love having my friends here, but I get uncalm if they arrive for drinks and I have to watch the potatoes boiling, so I try to serve things that don't need watching. I have a chicken and ham casserole I like to do. It wasn't supposed to be a chicken and ham casserole, it was supposed to be Shrimp Harpin. I had the Stratford gang here after they had finished a tour. I thumbed through recipe books looking for something to make and I came across this one for Shrimp Harpin. Because it looked fine in the book, I decided to do it. When I couldn't get any shrimp that day, I used chicken and ham instead.

"It turned out to be quite a deceptive dish. You see, I also forgot to put in the wine the recipe called for and I didn't realize it until one of the guests asked me what kind of wine I had used."

Grant Macdonald has been interested in food for a long time. One of his happiest commissions was in 1937, when he was asked to do drawings of the maîtres d'hôtel and chefs of the Savoy Hotel in London for use on the hotel's Christmas card.

"A room in the hotel was arranged as my studio. I had sittings every day for a week, with unforgettable interludes at noon when each of my subjects presided over the selection and presentation of one of his dishes for me. Then one morning I was served breakfast. I expressed appreciation of the superb omelette whereupon the chef asked if I had ever made one. Being brash enough to admit that I had tried to, he asked for my recipe which he remarked was quite perfect . . . except for one thing. Pepper!

" 'Never put pepper into anything before cooking because it turns rancid upon being subjected to heat,' he told me. 'Put it on after, and then freshly ground.'

"Since my recipe was otherwise 'quite perfect' there was no danger of my asking him for his recipe, and that tactic quite charmed me. He also told me that it was not possible to achieve a fine omelette in North America because the chickens spend too much time in the sun. This I took as an attempt to discourage any rivalry on my part when I returned to Canada."

Sylvia's Cake
1977

Grant Macdonald
1977-8

Chicken and Ham Casserole

½ pound (250g)	cooked chicken, coarsely chopped
½ pound (250g)	cooked ham, coarsely chopped
2 Tbsp (25mL)	lemon juice
2 Tbsp (25mL)	olive oil
2 Tbsp (25mL)	butter
½ pound (250g)	mushrooms, sliced
¼ cup (50mL)	chopped green pepper
½	Spanish onion, finely chopped
2 cups (500mL)	cooked rice
2 Tbsp (25mL)	finely chopped preserved ginger
2 Tbsp (25mL)	tomato paste
½ cup (125mL)	chicken stock
1 cup (250mL)	whipping cream
1 Tbsp (15mL)	liquid honey
	salt and pepper
½ cup (125mL)	toasted almond slivers
½ cup (125mL)	dry sherry

Combine chicken and ham in a small bowl. Sprinkle with lemon juice and set aside.

Heat olive oil and butter in a heavy frying pan. Sauté mushrooms, green pepper, and onion until tender. Stir in cooked rice, chopped ginger, tomato paste dissolved in chicken stock, whipping cream, and honey. Add chicken and ham and mix together thoroughly. Add salt and pepper to taste.

Spoon into a 2½-quart (2.5-L) casserole dish. Sprinkle top with almonds.

Bake at 350°F (180°C) uncovered for 40 to 50 minutes. Add sherry during final 20 minutes of cooking time.

Serves 4

Moussaka

2 Tbsp (25mL)	olive oil
1 pound (500g)	ground beef or lamb
1	Spanish onion, finely chopped
2	garlic cloves, crushed
½ pound (250g)	sliced mushrooms
6	plum tomatoes, peeled, seeded, and chopped
¼ cup (50mL)	chopped parsley
2 Tbsp (25mL)	tomato paste
½ cup (125mL)	beef stock
	salt and pepper
2	eggplants
	olive oil
½ cup (125mL)	Parmesan cheese
2	eggs
2 Tbsp (25mL)	flour
2 cups (500mL)	natural yoghurt

Heat olive oil in a heavy frying pan. Add beef, onion, garlic, and mushrooms and sauté until brown. Stir in tomatoes, parsley, and tomato paste diluted in beef stock. Add salt and pepper to taste. Cover and simmer for 10 minutes.

Meanwhile, wash eggplant but do not peel. Discard stem end. Slice thinly lengthwise. Brush lightly with olive oil and broil until golden on both sides.

Grease an 8-inch by 12-inch (3-L) baking pan. Line bottom with a layer of eggplant slices, overlapping them slightly. Cover with a layer of meat sauce. Sprinkle with Parmesan cheese. Repeat until all ingredients are used, ending with eggplant. Cover with a sauce made from whisking together the eggs, flour, and yoghurt. Sprinkle with more Parmesan cheese. Bake uncovered at 350°F (180°C) for 40 minutes.

Serves 6

Grant Macdonald, *Sylvia's Cake,* 1978. Acrylic on paper, 50.8 cm × 38.1 cm. Collection of Sylvia Rosen, Kingston. Photo: Gerry Locklin.

Lasagna

2 Tbsp (25mL)	olive oil
1 pound (500g)	ground beef
1	garlic clove, crushed
2 Tbsp (25mL)	chopped onion
8	plum tomatoes, peeled, seeded, and chopped
1 tsp (5mL)	basil
1 tsp (5mL)	oregano
1 tsp (5mL)	salt
	freshly ground pepper
1 Tbsp (15mL)	liquid honey
½ pound (250g)	wide spinach noodles, cooked
1 cup (250mL)	Parmesan cheese
2 cups (500mL)	ricotta or dry cottage cheese

Heat olive oil in a heavy frying pan. Add beef, garlic, and onion. Sauté until brown. Add tomatoes, basil, oregano, salt, pepper, and honey.

Grease an 8-inch by 12-inch (3-L) baking pan. Line bottom with a layer of cooked noodles. Sprinkle with Parmesan cheese. Cover with a layer of meat sauce and then a layer of ricotta cheese. Alternate layers, ending with a layer of meat sauce. Sprinkle generously with Parmesan cheese. Bake uncovered at 400°F (200°C) for 25 minutes.

Serves 6

Grant's Salad

1	large head Romaine lettuce
1 Tbsp (15mL)	French olive oil

Dressing

⅓ cup (75mL)	French olive oil
2 Tbsp (25mL)	wine vinegar
1	garlic clove, crushed
1 Tbsp (15mL)	liquid honey
	freshly ground sea salt and pepper

Wash lettuce. Roll leaves in paper towels and refrigerate until serving time. Break leaves into small pieces and toss with a spoonful of olive oil. Mix dressing. Pour over Romaine and toss.

Serves 4

Sylvia's Cake

1 box	Lemon Supreme cake mix
1 package	instant lemon pudding
¾ cup (175mL)	warm water
½ cup (125mL)	vegetable oil
1 tsp (5mL)	lemon extract
1 tsp (5mL)	almond extract
4	eggs
⅓ cup (75mL)	poppy seeds
⅓ cup (75mL)	rum

Grease a bundt or angel food pan well.

Combine cake mix and pudding mix in large bowl of electric mixer. Add water and oil and beat at low speed until combined. Add extracts and eggs, one at a time, continuing to beat for 4 minutes. Stir in poppy seeds. Pour into prepared pan. Bake at 350°F (180°C) for 50 to 60 minutes. Turn out onto a wire rack to cool. Sprinkle with rum.

Brandied Peaches

4 pounds (2kg)	peaches
4 cups (1L)	honey
4 cups (1L)	water
	brandy

Remove skin from peaches. Combine honey and water. Bring to a boil. Add peaches. Cover and simmer for 10 minutes. Spoon peaches into sterilized sealer jars. Cover with syrup until three-quarters full. Fill to the brim with brandy. Seal jars tightly.

Store in a cool dark place for at least 2 months before serving.

Yield: 4 quarts (4L)

Liz Magor, *Time and Mrs. Tiber,* 1976. Wood, glass, preserves, metal, paper, cardboard, 214.6 cm × 90.5 cm × 32.4 cm. Collection of the National Gallery of Canada, Ottawa.

Photo: Robert Keziere

Liz Magor

Liz Magor and her husband Don Worobey divide their time between their Vancouver home and Refuge Cove along the coast of British Columbia, where they live in a co-operative arrangement with a group of friends. There they cook on a wood stove and often it's some treat they've caught while sailing.

"There is such an abundance of fish there," says Liz. "Prawns, lobster, clams, oysters, and so on. I don't cook anything very fancy, probably because all this fabulous fish that surrounds us is so good when it's prepared in a simple way.

"Besides, for me, it's a luxury to take the time to cook. If I do, I'll rely on recipes from *Fanny Farmer* or *The Joy of Cooking*. But Don is much more imaginative and inventive than I. It's he who devised the Salmon à la Poof recipe."

Don likes cooking and gives explicit instructions—the number of charcoal briquets to use on the hibachi or the length of time to let something rest in mid-preparation ("about two cigarettes and a beer").

This past summer was one long culinary feast for the co-op. "We had lots of salmon this summer. Don caught two big white springs up the Toba Inlet. It was very exciting. I was steering. We've never caught such a big fish. It was like pulling a horse into the boat—even bent our net. We smoked one and canned the other.

"Also we were excited to find that Mr. Olivieri of Olivieri's Pasta Shop was visiting the cove on a boat. He was very flattered that we were all such big fans of his place on Commercial Drive and sent up eighty pounds of pasta and sauces—tortellini, spinach, ravioli, capeletti, and both meat sauces and pesto. We ate very well this summer."

Tiber Bay Salmon à la Poof

1 5-pound (2.5-kg)	salmon
	coarse salt
	brown sugar
	freshly ground pepper

Butterfly the fish by scraping away the flesh from the bone cage and back bone, starting at the belly. Take care not to cut through the skin. Place fish, skin side up, wipe with a damp cloth and then dry with paper towels.

Sprinkle with coarse salt, brown sugar, and freshly ground pepper. Pat coating into a thin crust. Set aside for 30 minutes.

Prepare barbecue or hibachi. When coals are ready, spread them out evenly, covering an area as large as the fish. Cover with green alder or other hardwood twigs.

Prepare a poof (cover) of heavy-duty aluminum foil, large enough to cover the fish and hibachi or barbecue completely.

Place fish on a well-greased grill, skin side down. Set grill about 4 inches (10cm) above the coals and quickly seal the hibachi or barbecue with the prepared poof, leaving plenty of space above the fish to allow heat and smoke to circulate.

Let cook for approximately 30 minutes. When a smoky glaze has formed on the edges of the fish and white fat has oozed out and is sitting on the surface, it is done.

Serve with wild rice and a green salad.

Serves 6

Salmon en Croûte

6 4-ounce (125-g)	salmon fillets
	frozen puff pastry
	butter
	salt and pepper

	Sauce
1½ cups (375mL)	sliced mushrooms
6 Tbsp (75mL)	butter
3 Tbsp (40mL)	flour
2 cups (500mL)	cream
1 tsp (5mL)	dry mustard
	salt and pepper
¼ cup (50mL)	sherry

Wipe salmon fillets dry with paper towels.

Roll out puff pastry to ¼-inch (5-mm) thickness. Cut into pieces large enough to enclose fillets in an envelope shape. Place a fillet on each piece of pastry. Dot with butter and sprinkle with salt and pepper. Fold up pastry and moisten edges to seal. Place seam-side down on a greased baking sheet. Bake at 400°F (200°C) for 20 to 25 minutes.

To make the sauce, sauté the sliced mushrooms in 2 tablespoons (25mL) butter until golden. Set aside.

Melt 4 tablespoons (50mL) of the butter in a medium saucepan. Stir in flour, then slowly add cream. Add mustard, a sprinkling of salt and pepper, and sherry, stirring until mixture has thickened. Pour over salmon en croûte.

Serves 6

Jean McEwen

When Jean and Indra McEwen spent a year in France recently, where Jean was painting, their culinary creativity and capabilities were put to a severe test. They came out of it convinced that they could survive—and survive well—in any set of difficult circumstances.

The kitchen of their tiny Paris apartment consisted of a single-burner hot plate. Nothing more. "Everything we cooked came off that one burner," says Jean, "and we ate some spectacular meals and entertained friends too.

"Furthermore, I gained twenty-five pounds! The foods that one has access to are all so different in France—wonderful sausages and *charcuterie*, veal, rabbit, unheard-of fishes. And then there are the cheeses. No wonder I gained all that weight!"

Since returning to Canada, they have taken up residence in a gracious grey-stone townhouse whose large windows overlook Lafontaine Park in Montreal. Its kitchen is enormous, giving the McEwens plenty of space to cook together—an activity they greatly enjoy—and to house their large cookbook collection.

"We never work on the same dish together, though," explains Indra. "We each do separate things that make up the meal."

"And we have devised a system for evaluating the recipes," Jean says. "Something that is very good, and suitable for company, gets a four-star rating. Something that is okay, but not fantastic, gets three stars—the sort of thing we'd make again to serve the family. Something that is only good enough to rate two stars won't get repeated again, and we've never had anything that came out with only one star.

"What we've found with the system, is that we have a ready-made list of foods that we can put together into a delicious meal when we want to entertain. We don't have to spend a lot of time worrying about what to make because it's all here."

Bouillabaisse

½ pound (250g)	halibut
½ pound (250g)	cod
½ pound (250g)	bass
2	onions, coarsely chopped
2	tomatoes, peeled, seeded, and chopped
⅓ cup (75mL)	olive oil
1 tsp (5mL)	fennel seed
½ tsp (2mL)	thyme
½ tsp (2mL)	saffron
1 tsp (5mL)	salt
	freshly ground pepper
1	bay leaf
1 cup (250mL)	toasted croutons, as garnish
1 Tbsp (15mL)	chopped parsley, as garnish

Cut the fish in bite-sized pieces and place in a heavy saucepan along with all the remaining ingredients except the croutons and parsley. Add boiling water to cover and with the lid on, boil briskly for 15 minutes.

Serve in heated soup plates, garnished with croutons and chopped parsley.

Serves 4

Rabbit Stew

1 4-pound (2-kg)	rabbit (approx.)
½ cup (125mL)	diced pork fat or bacon
1 Tbsp (15mL)	butter
1 Tbsp (15mL)	olive oil
½ cup (125mL)	flour
2	onions, finely chopped
2	garlic cloves, crushed
1	bottle red Burgundy wine
2 cups (500mL)	chicken stock
	bouquet garni (bay leaf, thyme, celery stalk and parsley, tied together in cheesecloth)
1 Tbsp (15mL)	wine vinegar
	salt and pepper to taste

Cut rabbit into serving pieces. Wipe dry and set aside. In a heavy casserole, brown diced pork fat in butter and olive oil. When crisp, remove with a slotted spoon and set aside.

Roll rabbit pieces in flour, shaking to remove excess. Sauté in the fat remaining in the casserole until golden in colour. Remove and set aside.

Sauté the chopped onion and garlic until limp. Add wine and scrape up the bits clinging to the bottom of the pan. Return diced pork and rabbit to the casserole. Add chicken stock, *bouquet garni*, and vinegar. Bring to a boil, reduce heat and simmer, covered, for 1 hour or until meat is tender.

Taste for seasonings and add salt and pepper as necessary. Serve with boiled potatoes and French bread croutons which have been fried in olive oil. Sprinkle with parsley.

Serves 4

Osso Bucco

3 Tbsp (40mL)	butter
¼ cup (50mL)	olive oil
3 pounds (1.5kg)	veal shanks
	flour
2	onions, finely chopped
2	carrots, finely chopped
2	stalks celery, finely chopped
2	garlic cloves, crushed
½ cup (125mL)	white wine
3	tomatoes, peeled, seeded, and chopped
2 cups (500mL)	beef stock
1 tsp (5mL)	thyme
1 Tbsp (15mL)	chopped fresh parsley
1	bay leaf
	salt and pepper
2 tsp (10mL)	grated lemon rind
2	garlic cloves, crushed
¼ cup (50mL)	finely chopped parsley

Heat butter and oil in a heavy saucepan. Dredge veal shanks in flour and brown in hot oil. Remove from pan and set aside. Add onion, carrots, celery, and garlic to oil remaining in the pan. Sauté lightly. Add wine and scrape brown bits clinging to the bottom and sides of pan.

Stir in tomatoes, stock, thyme, 1 tablespoon (15mL) chopped parsley, and bay leaf. Add salt and pepper if desired.

Return veal shanks to pan. Bring to the boil, reduce heat, and simmer, covered, for 1 hour, adding more wine if necessary.

Just before serving, sprinkle with a mixture of lemon rind, crushed garlic, and ¼ cup (50mL) chopped parsley.

Serves 4

Cassoulet

3 pounds (1.5kg)	uncooked Polish sausage, cut in 2-inch (5-cm) lengths
1	jambonneau (French-style pressed ham) or 1 pound (500g) picnic shoulder ham, cut in chunks
2 cups (500mL)	lentils
2	onions, finely chopped
2	garlic cloves, crushed
	bouquet garni (bay leaf, thyme, celery stalk and parsley, tied together in cheesecloth)
2	cloves
1 tsp (5mL)	salt
	freshly ground pepper
6 cups (1.5L)	chicken stock (approx.)

Combine all ingredients in a heavy casserole, adding enough stock to cover the meat. Bring to the boil, cover, and simmer gently until lentils are tender—approximately 2 hours. If necessary, add more stock.

Just before serving, place under broiler to form a crisp topping.

Serves 8

Guido Molinari

Good cooking is a tradition in the Molinari family.

"From my mother I learned survival," says painter Guido Molinari. "She was an excellent cook who learned how to do things from her mother-in-law and she passed it on to her children."

The result is that, today, friendly rivalries exist in the Montreal kitchens of the now adult brothers and sisters. "We have contests to see who makes the best ravioli. I, of course, always win because mine is the best," he smiles.

As for his own family, it is frequently scattered. His wife, Fernande Saint-Martin, an art historian, is often away for long periods of time. Their two children are in their late teens and "pretty much take care of themselves." One of them eats macrobiotic food, which doesn't much interest Guido, who likes meat, "although never beef."

While Guido enjoys being creative in the kitchen, he doesn't take time to prepare anything extravagant when cooking only for himself. But if there is any special cooking to be done, it's Guido who does it.

"Fernande doesn't cook. She doesn't have to cook with all those degrees!"

Pasta

2 cups (500mL)	flour
1 tsp (5mL)	salt
4	eggs

Place flour and salt in a mound on kitchen counter or pastry board. Make a well in the centre and break the eggs into the well. Using a fork, beat eggs in a fluffing motion, slowly incorporating the flour at the inner edges of the mound. Use the other hand to shore up the edges of the mound if they start to cave in. When it becomes too difficult to continue with the fork, use the fingers to work the remaining flour into the egg to form a stiff, smooth dough. Not all flour may be used or a little more may be necessary.

Knead the dough until smooth. Cover with plastic wrap and let rest for 30 minutes. Breaking off small pieces at a time, roll out and cut into desired shapes or pass through pasta machine. Use for ravioli, canneloni, spaghetti, lasagna, and other pasta dishes.

Polpette—Neapolitan Meat Sauce

2 pounds (1kg)	ground veal
2 pounds (1kg)	ground pork
2 Tbsp (25mL)	olive oil
1	large onion, diced
¼ cup (50mL)	chopped parsley
½ cup (125mL)	diced celery
2	garlic cloves, crushed
2 tsp (10mL)	oregano
2 tsp (10mL)	basil
	salt and pepper
3 14-ounce (398-mL)	cans Italian plum tomatoes
2 5½-ounce (156-mL)	cans tomato paste

In a heavy frying pan, brown meat in olive oil. Add onion, parsley, celery, garlic, oregano, basil, salt and pepper. Cook, stirring until meat is browned.

Stir in the tomatoes and mix together well. Gradually add tomato paste. Cover and simmer for 1½ hours.

Yield: 2 quarts (2.25L) (approx.)

Ravioli

Stuffing	
1 cup (250mL)	grated Parmigiana cheese
1 cup (250mL)	grated Romano cheese
2	eggs, beaten
¼ cup (50mL)	chopped parsley
½ cup (125mL)	finely diced celery
½ cup (125mL)	finely chopped cooked spinach
1	garlic clove, crushed
2 Tbsp (25mL)	finely chopped red pepper
	salt and pepper
1 tsp (5mL)	oregano
1 tsp (5mL)	basil
1 tsp (5mL)	savory
	pasta
	Polpette

Mix all stuffing ingredients together and set aside.

Roll out pasta into a large thin sheet, approximately ⅛ inch (2.5mm) thick. Dot it with about 60 teaspoon-sized portions of stuffing, leaving about 2 inches (5cm) between mounds. Brush pasta with beaten egg. Top with a second sheet of thinly rolled pasta, easing it to fit over the mounds. Using a 1½-inch (3.5-cm) circle, cut out around the mounds of stuffing. Crimp the edges together carefully.

Drop into a large pot of salted boiling water. Cook for 7 to 10 minutes or until tender. Drain. To serve, simmer in Polpette for 30 minutes to heat through.

Yield: 5 dozen. Serves 6 to 8

Meat Balls

2 pounds (1kg)	ground veal
1 cup (250mL)	grated Parmigiana cheese
1 cup (250mL)	grated Romano cheese
2 cups (500mL)	fresh bread crumbs
¼ cup (50mL)	chopped parsley
½ cup (125mL)	chopped cooked spinach
2	garlic cloves, crushed
2 Tbsp (25mL)	finely chopped red pepper
1½ tsp (7mL)	salt
¼ tsp (1mL)	pepper
1 tsp (5mL)	oregano
1 tsp (5mL)	basil
1 tsp (5mL)	savory
3	eggs, beaten
	dry bread crumbs
	fat for deep frying

Mix all ingredients together, except dry bread crumbs and fat. Form into balls the size of a walnut and roll in dry bread crumbs. Deep fry in fat at a temperature of 375°F (190°C) for 8 to 10 minutes or until crisp and browned. Remove with a slotted spoon and drain on paper towels.

Simmer in Polpette for 30 minutes to heat through.

Serve with spaghetti noodles.

Yield: 9 dozen meat balls. With sauce and spaghetti, serves 8 to 10

Poultry Stuffing

1 cup (250mL)	grated Parmigiana cheese
1 cup (250mL)	grated Romano cheese
2 cups (500mL)	fresh bread crumbs
¼ cup (50mL)	chopped parsley
½ cup (125mL)	finely diced celery
½ cup (125mL)	chopped cooked spinach
1	garlic clove, crushed
2 Tbsp (25mL)	finely chopped red pepper
	salt and pepper
1 tsp (5mL)	oregano
1 tsp (5mL)	basil
1 tsp (5mL)	savory
3	beaten eggs

Mix all ingredients together. Makes enough to stuff one turkey.

Douglas Morton

"All but two of our six children are grown and gone from home so we're finally getting to eat the sorts of things we really want to," says Doug Morton. "Mickey is a very good cook, and while I enjoy cooking, it's rather a rare occasion when I do it."

Many of the recipes that Mickey Morton uses come from the hand-written cookbook that Doug's mother, Mary Murdoch Morton, kept adding to until her death more than twenty years ago. Old country recipes such as sweet milk scones, soda cake, boiled cake, Scottish shortbread, treacle pudding and Scottish potted meat, reflect the elder Mrs. Morton's background. They remain family favourites two generations later.

"She was a very great lady, very religious and Christian in her ways," says Mickey. "She lived in the Winnipeg suburb of East Kildonan—one of the old Red River settlements. A few years ago, the little church she worked so hard for named a prayer room after her. And she was an excellent cook."

"I remember cooking with my mother when we spent summers at Lake of the Woods. I'd go out and catch fresh fish and bring it home for supper and help her prepare it," Doug recalls over a cup of coffee at York University, where he now teaches painting.

"Nowadays, though, I like things like raw oysters and moose, which are a long way from shortbread and bannock!"

Whole Wheat Scones

3 cups (750mL)	whole wheat flour
1 cup (250mL)	white flour
1 Tbsp (15mL)	sugar
1 tsp (5mL)	salt
1 tsp (5mL)	baking soda
1½ tsp (7mL)	cream of tartar
¼ cup (50mL)	shortening
2¼ cups (550mL)	milk

Mix the dry ingredients together in a large bowl. Cut in the shortening with a pastry blender or 2 knives. Using a fork, stir in enough milk to form a stiff dough. Divide in 2 pieces. Flatten each into a circle 9 inches (22cm) in diameter. Cut each piece in 6 wedges. Place wedges 2 inches (5cm) apart on a greased baking sheet. Bake at 450°F (230°C) for 10 to 15 minutes.

Yield: 1 dozen

Gingerbread

1 cup (250mL)	shortening
1 cup (250mL)	sugar
2	eggs
¾ cup (175mL)	molasses
2 tsp (10mL)	ginger
2 tsp (10mL)	cinnamon
1 tsp (5mL)	baking soda
1 cup (250mL)	boiling water
3 cups (750mL)	flour

Cream shortening with sugar until light and fluffy. Add eggs, molasses, ginger, and cinnamon.

Dissolve baking soda in boiling water and add to shortening mixture. Beat in flour.

Pour into greased 8-inch by 12-inch (3-L) pan. Bake at 350°F (180°C) for 35 to 40 minutes.

Oatmeal Shortbread

1 cup plus 2 Tbsp (250mL)	butter
1 cup (250mL)	brown sugar
1½ cups (375mL)	flour
½ tsp (2mL)	baking powder
¼ tsp (1mL)	nutmeg
1½ cups (375mL)	rolled oats

Cream butter. Add sugar and beat until light and fluffy.

Sift together the flour, baking powder, and nutmeg. Add to butter mixture. Stir in rolled oats.

Roll out on a floured surface to ¼-inch (5-mm) thickness. Cut in 2-inch (5-cm) circles. Place on greased baking pans.

Chill for 30 minutes. Bake at 350°F (180°C) for 10 to 12 minutes.

Yield: 5 dozen

Molly Morgan's Shortbread

1 pound (454g)	unsalted butter, at room temperature
1 cup (250mL)	fruit sugar
4 cups (1L)	flour

Cream butter until light and fluffy. Very gradually add sugar, a tablespoon at a time. Gradually add flour. Form into 2 balls and chill for 30 minutes.

Roll out to ¼-inch (5-mm) thickness. Cut in 2-inch (5-cm) circles. Place on ungreased baking pans.

Chill for 30 minutes. Bake at 325°F (160°C) for 25 to 30 minutes.

Yield: 6 dozen

Date Bars

2	egg yolks
1 cup (250mL)	confectioners sugar
⅔ cup (175mL)	flour
¼ tsp (1mL)	salt
2 tsp (10mL)	baking powder
1 tsp (5mL)	vanilla
1 cup (250mL)	chopped walnuts
1 cup (250mL)	chopped dates
2	egg whites, stiffly beaten

Beat egg yolks until thick and lemon coloured. Gradually add sugar. Sift together the flour, salt, and baking powder, and add to the egg yolks. Mix in vanilla, nuts, and dates. Fold in stiffly beaten egg whites.

Spread batter in a well-greased 8-inch by 12-inch (3-L) cake pan.

Bake at 350°F (180°C) for 20 to 25 minutes. Cut while warm.

Yield: 28 squares

Jelly Roll

6	eggs
1 cup (250mL)	sugar
1 cup (250mL)	flour
4 tsp (20mL)	baking powder
1 tsp (5mL)	salt
1 tsp (5mL)	vanilla
	jam or jelly
	confectioners sugar

Beat eggs until thick and lemon coloured. Gradually add sugar. Sift together the flour, baking powder, and salt and add it to the eggs. Stir in vanilla.

Grease a 15-inch by 10-inch by ¾-inch (2-L) jelly roll pan and line with waxed paper. Grease again. Pour in batter, spreading evenly.

Bake at 375°F (190°C) for 12 to 15 minutes.

Remove from oven and invert onto a clean towel that has been dusted with sifted confectioners sugar. Peel off paper. Cool. Trim off crusty edges. Spread with jam or jelly. Roll up starting with a short end. Place seam side down on a plate. Dust with confectioners sugar.

Sour Cream Chocolate Cake

2	egg yolks
1 cup (250mL)	sugar
2 squares	unsweetened chocolate, melted
1 cup (250mL)	cake flour
1 tsp (5mL)	baking powder
¼ tsp (1mL)	salt
1 cup (250mL)	commercial sour cream
½ tsp (2mL)	baking soda
1 tsp (5mL)	vanilla
2	egg whites, stiffly beaten

Beat the egg yolks until thick and lemon coloured. Gradually add sugar. Stir in melted chocolate.

Sift together the flour, baking powder, and salt. Add to the eggs alternately with the sour cream to which the baking soda has been added. Add vanilla and fold in beaten egg whites.

Pour into a well-greased 9-inch square (2.5-L) cake pan. Bake at 350°F (180°C) for 25 to 30 minutes.

Rich English Fruit Cake

1 pound (454g)	butter
1 pound (454g)	sugar
10	eggs
1 pound (454g)	flour
1 tsp (5mL)	nutmeg
¼ pound (100g)	almond pieces
1 pound (500g)	dried currants
1 pound (500g)	sultana raisins
½ pound (250g)	mixed candied peel
½ pound (250g)	candied cherries

Cream the butter until light and fluffy. Gradually add sugar. Beat in eggs, one at a time. Sift flour and nutmeg together. Save 1 cup (250mL) to toss fruits with, then add remaining flour to batter.

Combine fruits. Toss with reserved flour. Add to batter.

Grease, line with brown paper, and grease again, a 9-inch square (2.5-L) cake pan and a 6-inch square (1.5-L) cake pan.

Divide batter between the two.

Bake at 300°F (150°C) for 2 hours for smaller pan, for 2½ hours for larger pan.

Yield: 2 cakes

Gary Olson

While painter Gary Olson was growing up in Minnesota, the adults in his family were sowing the seeds for his future of serious food appreciation.

"Both my mother and my Aunt Olive were great cooks. On the whole, I had a basic meat-and-potatoes upbringing, except for desserts, because that's where they got really creative," he says, identifying the root of his sweet tooth, which survives to this day.

"When I was a child, Aunt Olive lived on a farm, and she made, among other things, the greatest doughnuts. She did a lot of baking—mostly recipes from church-guild cookbooks. I remember she picked blueberries every summer and made everything with them—jams, sauces, pies, cakes, muffins—you name it. They went into everything!"

Although long gone from Minnesota and the bounty of Aunt Olive's kitchen—except during annual summer visits—Gary's favourite foods are still desserts and sweets. He admits to a diet that is about half health food and half junk food. "The taste, texture, smell, and appearance of food are all important to me," he says, "but still, I'll look for any excuse to have some sweets. I love Swedish pancakes on a Sunday morning."

Now living in Cochrane, near Calgary, he and his wife Jill are surrounded by friends who also enjoy cooking and eating good food. They get together frequently with artist colleagues Derek Besant, Sandy Haeseker, and Lyndal Osborne, who delight in serving each other exciting and exotic fare. They once shared preparations for a dinner honouring a visiting artist, and produced a greatly assorted feast. It was

climaxed with Derek Besant's dessert cake—an enormous effort decorated with an icing face compressed by a piece of plexiglass. "The visual effect was staggering, and the taste sensation was stupendous," they say.

The Olson sweet tooth loves to sink itself into ice cream, particularly the home-made variety. A hand-cranked ice-cream maker often gets called into action when the group gets together and everybody takes a turn on it. "But the best reward is the ice cream at the end—pure 'Cholesterol City,' " Gary muses, his eyes glazing over at the memory.

Gary Olson, *Lunchtime in my Studio,* 1980. Graphite
and colour pencil on paper, 76.2 cm × 101.6 cm.
Collection of the artist.

Jill's Swedish Pancakes

1 cup (250mL)	flour
½ tsp (2mL)	salt
1 tsp (5mL)	sugar
4	egg yolks
1 cup (250mL)	milk
3 Tbsp (40mL)	natural yoghurt
4	egg whites, stiffly beaten

Sift together the flour, salt, and sugar. Set aside.

Beat egg yolks until thick and lemon coloured. Add to dry ingredients alternately with milk. Stir in yoghurt. Fold in beaten egg whites.

Spoon onto hot greased griddle. Cook until underside is brown and bubbles form on surface. Turn. Cook briefly on other side.

Serve with Aunt Olive's Blueberry Sauce

Yield: 2 dozen 4-inch (6-cm) pancakes

Aunt Olive's Blueberry Sauce

6 cups (1.5L)	fresh blueberries
1 cup (250mL)	sugar
2 cups (500mL)	water

Combine all ingredients and boil gently for 10 minutes.

Yield: 8 cups (2L)

Arlene's Banana Bread

3 cups (750mL)	sugar
1 cup (250mL)	vegetable oil
4	eggs
1 cup (250mL)	sour milk
2 tsp (10mL)	vanilla
6 cups (1.5L)	whole wheat flour
1 tsp (5mL)	salt
2 tsp (10mL)	baking soda
1 cup (250mL)	chopped walnuts
6	small ripe bananas, mashed

Combine sugar and oil. Add eggs, beating well. Blend in milk and vanilla. Add flour, salt and baking soda and mix together thoroughly.

Stir in walnuts and mashed bananas.

Pour batter into 3 greased loaf pans. Bake at 350°F (180°C) for 1 hour.

Yield: 3 loaves

Heart Attack Ice Cream

1¼ cups (300mL)	sugar
¼ tsp (1mL)	salt
12	egg yolks
2 quarts (2L)	whipping cream
2 Tbsp (25mL)	vanilla

Beat sugar, salt, and egg yolks until thick. Gradually add whipping cream and vanilla. Pack into an ice cream maker and freeze.

Yield: 4 quarts (4L)

Berrie Ice Cream

1½ cups (375mL)	sugar
¼ tsp (1mL)	salt
6	egg yolks
1 quart (1L)	half-and-half cream
1 quart (1L)	whipping cream
3 cups (750mL)	fresh berries of your choice (raspberries, strawberries or blueberries)
6	egg whites

Combine 1 cup (250mL) of the sugar with the salt and egg yolks. Beat well. Scald half-and-half cream. Gradually add to egg yolk mixture. Set aside to cool thoroughly. Stir in whipping cream.

Wash and slightly mash berries. Add to egg yolk mixture. Beat egg whites until stiff peaks form. Beat in remaining ½ cup (125mL) sugar. Add to egg and cream mixture. Pack into ice cream maker and freeze.

Yield: 4 quarts (4L)

Aunt Olive's Apple Pie Cake

¼ cup (50mL)	butter
1 cup (250mL)	sugar
1	egg
¼ tsp (1mL)	salt
1 tsp (5mL)	cinnamon
½ tsp (2mL)	nutmeg
1 tsp (5mL)	baking soda
1 cup (250mL)	flour
½ cup (125mL)	chopped walnuts or raisins
2½ cups (625mL)	diced apples
2 Tbsp (25mL)	hot water
1 tsp (5mL)	vanilla

Cream butter and sugar until light and fluffy. Add egg and continue beating. Stir in dry ingredients, combining thoroughly, then add walnuts, apples, water, and vanilla.

Grease a 9-inch (1-L) pie plate and pour in batter. Bake at 350°F (180°C) for 45 minutes.

Cut into wedges and serve with whipped cream or ice cream.

Mom's Hershey Pie

Crust

1 cup (250mL)	graham cracker crumbs
⅓ cup (75mL)	melted butter

Filling

½ cup (125mL)	milk
15	marshmallows
6 31-gram	Hershey almond bars
1 cup (250mL)	whipping cream, whipped

Combine cracker crumbs with melted butter and press into the bottom and sides of a 9-inch (1-L) pie plate.

Heat milk and marshmallows in top of double boiler. Stir until marshmallows melt. Break Hershey bars into small pieces and add to milk mixture, and stir to melt. Remove from heat and set aside to cool. Fold in whipped cream. Pour into prepared shell. Chill before serving.

Mother's Peanut Butter Company Bars

½ cup (125mL)	sugar
1 cup (250mL)	white corn syrup
1 cup (250mL)	peanut butter
4 cups (1L)	Rice Krispies
1 6-ounce (170-g)	package semi-sweet chocolate pieces

Bring sugar and corn syrup to a boil. Remove from heat and add peanut butter and Rice Krispies.

Press into a well-greased 9-inch by 13-inch (4-L) pan. Sprinkle with chocolate pieces and place in a warm oven. When chocolate has melted, spread it evenly over mixture. Cut into squares or bars.

Aunt Olive's Rye Bread

1 tsp	(5mL)	sugar
1 package		yeast
¼ cup	(50mL)	lukewarm water
¼ cup	(50mL)	brown sugar
¼ cup	(50mL)	molasses
1 Tbsp	(15mL)	salt
2 Tbsp	(25mL)	shortening
1½ cups	(375mL)	hot water
2½ cups	(625mL)	medium rye flour
2½ cups	(625mL)	white flour (approx.)

Dissolve sugar and yeast in warm water. Set aside for 10 minutes.

In a large bowl, combine brown sugar, molasses, salt, and shortening. Add hot water and stir until sugar is dissolved. Cool to lukewarm. Add rye flour and beat well. Add yeast mixture. Add white flour, a cup at a time, beating well. When dough becomes too thick and heavy to continue beating, turn out onto a floured board and knead in enough remaining flour to form a stiff dough. Knead until smooth and elastic. Shape dough into a ball and place in a large buttered bowl, turning dough so all sides are buttered. Cover with a towel and set to rise in a warm draft-free place until double in bulk, approximately 1½ hours.

Punch dough down and let rest for 15 minutes. Divide into 2 pieces. Knead each piece briefly. Form into 2 loaves and place in greased bread pans. Cover with a towel and let rise until double in bulk.

Bake at 350°F (180°C) for 1 hour. Cool on a wire rack.

Yield: 2 loaves

Aunt Olive's Date and Orange-Slice Bars

½ pound	(250g)	dates
½ cup	(125mL)	sugar
2 Tbsp	(25mL)	flour
1 cup	(250mL)	water
¾ cup	(175mL)	shortening
1 cup	(250mL)	brown sugar
2		eggs
1 tsp	(5mL)	baking soda
2 tsp	(10mL)	hot water
1 tsp	(5mL)	vanilla
1¾ cups	(400mL)	flour
½ tsp	(2mL)	salt
½ cup	(125mL)	chopped nuts
1 15-ounce	(400-g)	package orange-slice candy

Combine dates, sugar, flour, and water in a heavy saucepan. Bring to a boil and cook until thick. Set aside to cool.

Cream shortening and brown sugar until light and fluffy. Beat in eggs. Add baking soda dissolved in hot water and vanilla. Stir in flour, salt, and nuts.

Spread half of batter in a greased 8-inch by 12-inch (3-L) pan. Cover with orange slices cut in thirds. Spread date mixture on top, then cover with remaining batter.

Bake at 350°F (180°C) for 40 minutes. Cut in squares.

Yield: 2 dozen squares

Aunt Olive's Fruit Cocktail Cookies

½ cup (125mL)	butter
½ cup (125mL)	shortening
1 cup (250mL)	brown sugar
½ cup (125mL)	white sugar
3	eggs
2 tsp (10mL)	vanilla
4 cups (1L)	flour
1 tsp (5mL)	baking powder
1 tsp (5mL)	baking soda
1 tsp (5mL)	salt
½ cup (125mL)	chopped pecans
¾ cup (175mL)	chopped walnuts
2 cups (500mL)	canned fruit cocktail, well drained

Cream the butter and shortening together until light and fluffy. Gradually add the brown and white sugar, eggs, and vanilla and beat well.

Sift together the flour, baking powder, baking soda, and salt. Combine with butter mixture. Stir in nuts and fruit cocktail.

Drop by teaspoonfuls onto a greased baking pan. Bake at 350°F (180°C) for 10 to 15 minutes. While still warm, glaze with frosting.

Frosting

4 Tbsp (50mL)	butter
1½ cups (375mL)	confectioners sugar
	warm water

Heat butter in a heavy saucepan until it is brown, taking care that it doesn't burn. Remove from heat. Add sugar. Add water until frosting reaches a spreading consistency.

Yield: 9 dozen cookies

Peanut Butter Cookies

1½ cups (375mL)	flour
1 tsp (5mL)	baking soda
1 tsp (5mL)	ginger
½ tsp (2mL)	cloves
¾ cup (175mL)	shortening
¾ cup (175mL)	chunky peanut butter
1 cup (250mL)	brown sugar
2	eggs
2 Tbsp (25mL)	milk
1 cup (250mL)	salted Spanish peanuts

Sift together the flour, baking soda, ginger, and cloves. Set aside.

Cream shortening and peanut butter until light and fluffy. Gradually add sugar, continuing to beat. Add eggs and milk. Gradually stir in sifted dry ingredients. Add peanuts.

Drop by teaspoon onto greased baking pan. Bake at 375°F (190°C) for 10 to 12 minutes.

Yield: 9 dozen

Arlene's Date Bread

1½ cups (375mL)	chopped dates
½ cup (125mL)	water
1 Tbsp (15mL)	sugar
1 cup (250mL)	sugar
2 Tbsp (25mL)	vegetable oil
1	beaten egg
1 cup (250mL)	boiling water
2 cups (500mL)	whole wheat flour
½ tsp (2mL)	baking soda
1 cup (250mL)	chopped walnuts

Cook the chopped dates, water and 1 tablespoon (15mL) sugar together until soft. Set aside to cool, then add remaining ingredients. Mix together well.

Pour batter into a greased loaf pan. Bake at 375°F (190°C) for 50 to 60 minutes.

Yield: 1 loaf

Toni Onley

For a long time, Toni Onley lived on a houseboat moored in Vancouver's Coal Harbour. It is important for him to be close to the sea.

"I was born on the Isle of Man and have lived on one ocean or another for most of my life. My father, who was a Shakespearean actor when he was not fishing, had a boat. We were good at fishing and during the hungry years of World War II we were often able to feed all our neighbours as well as ourselves. My mother would souse fish, dry fish, and salt fish for the long winters. Fish kept us alive."

So did his grandfather's vegetables. Grandfather had hothouses—seven miles of them eventually—("the longest hothouse in the British Commonwealth") in which he grew vegetables year round. "But still, because of the war, my sisters never saw bananas or other fruits until they were seven or eight."

In 1948 when he was in his late teens, Toni came to Canada, settling first in Ontario and then in British Columbia. Piloting his own plane, he now explores the North American continent, painting in water colours and photographing the bare landscapes he visits.

In 1978 he made his first trip to Japan with his fiancée, Yukiko. People said to him before he left, "You'll lose weight." "But I was an exception," he said. "I have been prepared all my life for Japanese cooking. I had already eaten raw fish, crossing that threshold long before going to Japan.

"Yukiko insisted I try everything from the local *okonomi-yake* (pancakes) to the most artistically arranged *kaiseki*, which is food for

Photo: Robert Keziere, Vancouver Art Gallery

special occasions, such as moon viewing in September. It is food designed to heighten sensations to the eyes, nose, and palate. Unfortunately, *kaiseki* can only be served in Japan, because without the 'right heart' there can be no true *kaiseki*."

Ichiban Dashi
Basic Soup Stock

10 cups (2.5L)	water
1 3-inch (8-cm)	square *kombu* (dried kelp)
1 cup (250mL)	flaked *katsuobushi* (dried bonito)

Bring water to the boil. Add *kombu*. Return water to the boil then immediately remove *kombu* from the water and set it aside. Stir in *katsuobushi*. Turn off heat. Let rest for 2 minutes or until *katsuobushi* sinks to the bottom of the pan.

Pour stock through a sieve lined with a double layer of cheesecloth into a clean bowl. Reserve the *katsuobushi*.

Stock may be used as a base for soup or for cooking. It may be kept for 2 days, refrigerated.

Yield: 2½ quarts (2.5L)

Niban Dashi
Cooking Stock for Vegetables

1 3-inch (8-cm)	square cooked *kombu* left over from *ichiban dashi*
1 cup (250mL)	cooked *katsuobushi* left over from *ichiban dashi*
5 cups (1.25L)	water
¼ cup (50mL)	flaked fresh *katsuobushi* (dried bonito)

Combine leftover *kombu* and leftover *katsuobushi* with cold water and bring to the boil. Add fresh *katsuobushi*, reduce heat and simmer, uncovered, for 5 minutes.

Pour stock through a sieve lined with a double layer of cheesecloth into a clean bowl. Discard the *kombu* and *katsuobushi*.

Stock may be used for cooking vegetables. It may be kept for 2 days, refrigerated.

Yield: 1¼ quarts (1.25L)

Sukiyaki

1 pound (500g)	tenderloin or sirloin steak
1	cup water
1 8-ounce (225-g)	can *shirataki* (noodle-like threads), drained
1 14-ounce (397-g)	can *takenoko* (bamboo shoot)
6	green onions, including some green stem cut into 1½-inch (4-cm) pieces
1	onion, cut in ¼-inch (5-mm) slices
6	mushrooms, sliced
2	tofu cakes (soybean curd), cut into 1-inch (2.5-cm) cubes
2 ounces (50g)	Chinese chrysanthemum leaves or watercress
2-inch (5-cm)	piece of beef fat

Sauce

¾ cup (175mL)	Japanese soy sauce
¼ cup (50mL)	sugar
¾ cup (175mL)	sake (rice wine)

Place beef in freezer for 30 minutes to make it easier to slice. Cut beef against the grain into ⅛-inch (2-mm) thick slices. Cut slices in half crosswise.

Boil water. Add *shirataki*. Return to boil. Drain. Cut noodles in half.

Cut bamboo shoot in half lengthwise then slice thinly crosswise. Run under cold water and drain.

Arrange meat, *shirataki*, vegetables and tofu in separate rows on a platter.

Combine sauce ingredients and set aside.

Preheat an electric frying pan to 425°F (220°C) or heat a heavy frying pan over high heat. Rub bottom of frying pan with piece of beef fat. Add half the meat and half the sauce and cook, stirring for 1 minute. Add half the vegetables and cook for an additional 4 or 5 minutes. Remove from pan and keep warm. Repeat with remaining meat and vegetables.

Serve with rice.

Serves 4

Misoshiru
Clear Soup with Soybean Paste

Aka Miso (summer soup)
6 cups (1.5L)	*ichiban dashi*
½ cup (125mL)	*aka miso* (red soybean paste)

Shiro Miso (winter soup)
6 cups (1.5L)	*ichiban dashi*
1 cup (250mL)	*shiro miso* (white soybean paste)

Awase Miso (combination *miso* soup)
6 cups (1.5L)	*ichiban dashi*
½ cup (125mL)	*shiro miso*
½ cup (125mL)	*aka miso*

To make any of the three soups, place *dashi* in a saucepan and set a sieve over it. Rub the *miso* through the sieve using the back of a large wooden spoon. Moisten with some *dashi* if necessary to help force it through.

Simmer for 2 minutes.

Pour into heated soup bowls, garnished with one of the three following garnishes, and serve immediately.

Serves 6

Garnishes

Tofu and Green Onion
1 6-ounce (175-g)	cake of tofu (soybean curd) cut into ¼-inch (5-mm) cubes
1	green onion, including green stem, cut into thin rounds

When soup has simmered, add tofu for 1 minute. Pour into soup bowls, garnish with green onion, and serve.

Daikon and Green Onion
1-inch (2.5-cm)	piece of *daikon* (Japanese white radish), peeled
1	green onion, including green stem, cut into thin rounds.

Cut the *daikon* into julienne strips about 2 inches (5cm) long. Cover the strips with cold water. Bring to the boil, covered, then reduce heat and simmer for 5 minutes. Drain. Add to simmering soup and serve. Garnish with green onion.

Fu and Mustard
18	*kohana-fu* or *yachiyo-fu* (pressed croutons)
1 tsp (5mL)	powdered mustard mixed with a little water

Soak the *kohana-fu* in cold water for 10 minutes. Squeeze to remove moisture. Add to simmering soup for 1 minute. Pour into soup bowls and add a drop of the mustard paste.

Kani Sunomono
Crab Meat in Vinegar Dressing

1	cucumber
½ cup (125mL)	cold water
1 tsp (5mL)	salt
12 ounces (340g)	fresh or canned crab meat
3 Tbsp (40mL)	grated fresh ginger root

Sambai-zu (rice vinegar and soy dipping sauce)
3 Tbsp (40mL)	rice vinegar
3 Tbsp (40mL)	*niban dashi* (see p. 150)
4 tsp (20mL)	sugar
2 tsp (10mL)	Japanese soy sauce
	pinch of salt

To make sauce, combine all ingredients and bring to the boil, stirring constantly. Remove from the heat and allow to cool to room temperature.

Partially peel cucumber lengthwise, leaving a few narrow strips of green skin to give colour. Cut cucumber in half lengthwise, remove seeds, and slice halves crosswise in thin slices.

Combine water and salt in a small bowl. Add cucumber and let soak for 30 minutes. Drain well, squeezing to remove all moisture.

Carefully pick over crab meat, discarding any cartilage and bone. Shred finely.

Divide cucumber and crab into 6 small dishes. Wrap grated ginger in a piece of cheesecloth and squeeze the juice of it over each dish.

Serve with dipping sauce.

Serves 6 as a first course

Tempura

	Soba Tsuyu (dipping sauce)
¼ cup (50mL)	mirin (sweet sake)
¼ cup (50mL)	Japanese soy sauce
1 cup (250mL)	niban dashi (see p. 150)
2 Tbsp (25mL)	katsuobushi (dried bonito)
pinch of	salt

1	small eggplant
18	canned ginnan (ginkgo nuts), drained
1 pound (500g)	raw shrimp, shelled and deveined
½ cup (125mL)	flour
12	snow peas
6	mushrooms, cut in half
1	sweet potato, peeled and cut into slices ¼ inch (5mm) thick vegetable oil

	Batter
1	egg yolk
2 cups (500mL)	cold water
¼ tsp (1mL)	baking soda
1⅔ cups (400mL)	flour

	Garnish
3 Tbsp (40mL)	finely grated daikon (Japanese white radish)
1 Tbsp (15mL)	grated fresh ginger root

To prepare dipping sauce, heat the *mirin* until lukewarm. Ignite with a match and shake pan until flame dies out. Stir in soy sauce, *niban dashi, katsuobushi,* and salt. Bring to the boil, strain through a fine sieve, and set aside to cool.

Peel the eggplant. Cut in half lengthwise then into ¼-inch (5-mm) slices. Wash in cold water and pat dry. Set aside.

Skewer 3 ginkgo nuts on each of 6 toothpicks. Set aside.

Sprinkle shrimp with flour. Shake to remove excess. Set all vegetables and shrimp in neat rows on a large platter.

To prepare batter, combine egg yolk with water. Add baking soda and flour and mix with a wooden spoon. Batter should be somewhat thin. It must be used immediately. Heat oil in a deep fryer or fondue pot to 375°F (190°C). Dip pieces of food in batter and drop into hot oil, frying until golden. Remove with slotted spoon or chopsticks and drain on paper towels. Continue frying until all ingredients are used.

Serve with garnish made by combining *daikon* and ginger root. Dip tempura in *soba tsuyu* (dipping sauce).

Serves 6

Teriyaki

	Teriyaki Sauce
1 cup (250mL)	mirin (sweet sake) or dry sherry
1 cup (250mL)	Japanese soy sauce
1 cup (250mL)	chicken stock

	Glaze
¼ cup (50mL)	teriyaki sauce
1 Tbsp (15mL)	sugar
2 tsp (10mL)	cornstarch
1 Tbsp (15mL)	cold water

1½ pounds (750g)	beef tenderloin or sirloin cut in 12 slices ¼ inch (5mm) thick

	Garnish
4 tsp (20mL)	dry mustard, mixed with a little water to form a paste parsley

Make the sauce by warming the *mirin.* Remove from the heat and ignite with a match. Shake the pan until the flame extinguishes itself. Add soy sauce and stock, bring to the boil, remove from the heat and set aside to cool.

Make the glaze by combining ¼ cup (50mL) *teriyaki* sauce and sugar in a saucepan. Bring to the boil then reduce heat and stir in cornstarch which has been mixed with water. Cook, stirring until mixture thickens. Pour into a bowl and set aside.

Preheat broiler. Dip beef slices in remaining *teriyaki* sauce and broil 2 inches from heat for 1 minute on each side. Remove to plates and cover with a little of the glaze. Garnish with a dab of mustard and a parsley sprig.

Serves 4

Lyndal Osborne, *Tumbled Pitas,* 1975. Air brush
drawing, 96.5 cm × 106.7 cm. Collection of Gary
Olson, Cochrane.

Lyndal Osborne

"I really like food," says painter Lyndal Osborne.

"I like it for its own sake, but I also like using food in my work. For the past five years, I have been using an air brush technique, and much of my subject material has been food. I find it interesting from a visual standpoint."

Having grown up on the coast of Australia, Lyndal's early food experiences centred around fresh fish and local vegetables. "We ate lots of pure, natural stuff, but I didn't really have any feeling for food then.

"After I grew up, I remember being really uncomfortable about going to a restaurant to eat. I actually said to a boyfriend, 'You're not going to waste your money on food in there are you?' At that time, I didn't see food as a social activity. It took me a couple of years to understand this aspect of eating, and now I realize that some of the most pleasurable experiences in my life happened over food."

Being an organized person, Lyndal finds entertaining an enjoyable activity, not a chore. "Bill, the man I live with, and I like to do dinner parties where we work like crazy on preparations for thirty minutes, and then we go out for a run before the guests arrive.

"But we also spend a lot of time together in the kitchen, and we work well together. We like spicy foods and using things like soy sauce and black beans and other hot stuff. One summer we made a salad every single day using only the fresh things we had growing in our garden. We have twenty or thirty meals down pat and some of them are spectacular—you know, the sorts of things your guests 'ooh and aah' at when you set them on the table. And we're constantly adding to our repertoire."

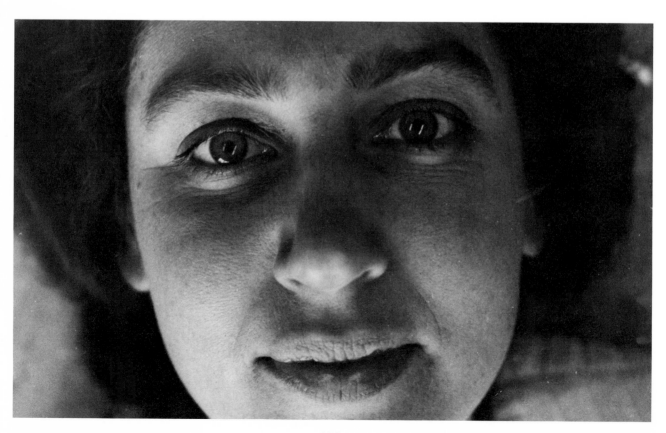

Curried Scallops

1 pound (500g)	scallops
¼ tsp (1mL)	salt
⅓ cup (75mL)	fine dry bread crumbs
¼ cup (50mL)	butter
1 tsp (5mL)	curry powder
2 tsp (10mL)	lemon juice
	lemon wedges or slices, as garnish
	parsley sprigs, as garnish

Wash scallops well and dry with paper towels. Mix salt and bread crumbs and coat scallops evenly.

Divide scallops among 6 shell baking dishes.

Melt butter, add curry powder and stir over medium heat for 2 minutes. Add lemon juice. Drizzle over scallops. Bake at 450°F (230°C) for 15 minutes. Garnish with lemon wedges or slices and with parsley sprigs.

Serves 6

Caesar Salad

1	garlic clove, crushed
¼ cup (50mL)	olive oil
1 head	Romaine lettuce
¼ tsp (1mL)	salt
	freshly ground pepper
1	coddled egg
	juice of half a lemon
4	anchovy fillets, chopped
¼ cup (50mL)	grated Parmesan cheese
1 cup (250mL)	croutons

Combine garlic and olive oil a day ahead and let stand to mingle flavours. Wash and dry lettuce. Break into small pieces. Toss with salt and pepper.

Pour in olive oil mixture and toss, then add coddled egg and lemon juice. Toss to coat leaves well. Add anchovies, cheese, and croutons and toss thoroughly.

Serves 6

Spaghetti Squash

2 10-inch (25-cm)	spaghetti squash
2 Tbsp (25mL)	butter
	salt and pepper
1	garlic clove, crushed

Cut squash in half lengthwise. Scoop out seeds. Dot with butter. Season with salt, pepper, and crushed garlic. Place, cut side up, in a shallow baking dish to which has been added half an inch (1cm) hot water. Cover with aluminum foil. Bake at 350°F (180°C) for 1½ hours.

To serve, scoop out pulp with a fork and mound in serving dish.

Serves 6

Lobster in Crêpes with Wine and Cheese Sauce

Crêpes

1 cup (250mL)	water
1 cup (250mL)	milk
4	eggs
½ tsp (2mL)	salt
1½ cups (375mL)	instant blending flour
4 Tbsp (50mL)	melted butter

Mix all ingredients together in a blender. Cover and set aside for 2 hours before using.

Lightly butter a 10-inch (25-cm) crêpe pan. Heat. Pour in about ¼ cup (50mL) batter. Quickly tilt pan to swirl batter evenly over the bottom. Pour off excess. Cook over medium-high heat until brown on the underside. Turn crêpe over and cook for a further 30 seconds or until lightly browned. Continue until all batter is used, stacking cooked crêpes on a wire rack.

Yield: 18 crêpes

Creamed Lobster

2 Tbsp (25mL)	butter
3 Tbsp (40mL)	minced green onion
1½ cups (375mL)	diced cooked lobster
	salt and pepper
¼ cup (50mL)	dry white vermouth

Heat butter in a heavy frying pan. Add remaining ingredients and cook, stirring over medium heat, until most of the vermouth has evaporated. Scrape into a bowl and set aside.

Wine and Cheese Sauce

⅓ cup (75mL)	dry white vermouth
2 Tbsp (25mL)	cornstarch mixed with 2 Tbsp (25mL) milk
1½ cups (375mL)	whipping cream
¼ tsp (1mL)	salt
	freshly ground pepper
½ cup (125mL)	grated Swiss cheese

Boil vermouth in a heavy saucepan until reduced to 1 tablespoon (15mL). Remove from heat and stir in cornstarch mixture, cream, and seasonings. Cook over medium heat, stirring, for 2 minutes. Add half the cheese. Stir to melt.

Transfer half the cheese sauce to the lobster mixture. Combine thoroughly and divide among crêpes. Roll up crêpes and arrange seam side down in a lightly buttered baking dish. Pour remaining sauce over crêpes. Sprinkle with remaining cheese. Bake at 425°F (220°C) for 15 to 20 minutes.

Serves 6

Fruits in Ginger Sauce

½ cup (125mL)	freshly squeezed orange juice
1 Tbsp (15mL)	sugar
1 Tbsp (15mL)	lemon juice
2 Tbsp (25mL)	dark rum
1 Tbsp (15mL)	minced crystallized ginger
1	cantaloupe melon
2	bananas
1 pint (500mL)	fresh strawberries

Combine orange juice, sugar, and lemon juice in a saucepan. Bring to the boil, cover, reduce heat, and simmer for 20 minutes. Stir in rum and ginger. Chill.

At serving time, scoop out cantaloupe with a melon baller. Mix with banana slices and hulled strawberries. Combine with syrup. Serve in compote dishes.

Serves 6

Joyce Wieland, *Arctic Passion Cake* (detail), 1971. Set
piece, 101.6 cm × 167.6 cm. Collection of the National
Gallery of Canada, Ottawa.

Charles Pachter, *Life Is Not A Fountain,* 1977.
Acrylic and latex on canvas, 182 cm × 304 cm.
Collection of the artist.

Charles Pachter

"Like anything else in life, if you're willing to take risks, it can be spectacular," says Charles Pachter, referring to his famous Atomic Salad.

He began experimenting with it as a student in France, and over the years it has evolved into its present form. There seems little likelihood of its ever reaching a state of perfection or a level of boredom, however, because Charlie is flexible in making it, insisting only that the order of mixing it together is important.

"You can add to it or subtract from it, depending on how you feel, but you have to put it together in a certain sequence. Some of the ingredients—the basic ones—must be allowed to marinate in the oils and herbs in order to bring out their full flavour. Some things must be tossed in at the last moment so they won't get soggy. And you should never use iceberg lettuce. It's boring."

Charlie is an aesthete when it comes to food. "The same aesthetic considerations that go into a painting should go into the preparation of food," he says.

He is constantly receptive to culinary inspirations, just as he is to inspirations for his paintings. Many of his sources are reflected in the names he gives to his culinary creations. Frank the Pirate's Wife's Chicken was inspired by the wife of a used-car dealer in Guelph. The Dishwasher Fish came about from his having heard that cooking by this means was possible. (He tried it for himself and met with success.) "But you must have the type of dishwasher that has a boosted heat cycle, otherwise you'll have to cook it the conventional way in the oven," he says.

While his friends in Toronto clamour for the Atomic Salad, he enjoys creating other dishes for them as well. And although he likes cooking for a lot of people, he also enjoys experimenting for his own enjoyment.

"I'm always mixing things together. It doesn't matter if company is coming. I check what's fresh at the market, or at my farm, or what I have in the fridge, and then I decide what can be made with it. I love cooking, and even more, I love eating. It's fun to do with friends."

Atomic Salad

1	garlic clove, peeled
4 Tbsp (50mL)	apple cider vinegar
1 tsp (5mL)	salt
½ tsp (2mL)	pepper
1 tsp (5mL)	Dijon-style mustard
½ cup (125mL)	olive oil
1	large tomato, cut in wedges
1	avocado, sliced
½ cup (125mL)	sliced mushrooms
½ cup (125mL)	Mozzarella cheese, cut in small cubes
2	pepperoni, cut in ½-inch (1-cm) slices
8	large black olives
1 cup (250mL)	artichoke hearts, cut in halves
1	onion, sliced into thin rings
2 heads	Boston lettuce

Rub wooden salad bowl with peeled garlic. Toss remaining ingredients, except for the lettuce, in bowl. Mix together well. Let sit for 1 to 2 hours.

Separate leaves from Boston lettuce. Wash and dry thoroughly. Add to salad bowl at serving time. Toss well.

Serves 6

Glazed Beef

1 4-pound (2-kg)	sirloin tip roast
2	garlic cloves, peeled and cut in slivers
½ cup (125mL)	tomato sauce
1 tsp (5mL)	salt
	freshly ground pepper
1 Tbsp (15mL)	molasses
1 Tbsp (15mL)	soy sauce
2 tsp (10mL)	powdered ginger
1 tsp (5mL)	dry mustard
1 tsp (5mL)	brown sugar
1 tsp (5mL)	anchovy sauce or paste

Pierce the roast in several places with the tip of a sharp knife and insert garlic slivers.

Combine remaining ingredients. Brush entire roast with this sauce. Bake at 450°F (230°C) for 15 minutes. Lower heat to 275°F (140°C) and cook for a further 2 hours. Adjust time according to preference for rare, medium or well done.

Serves 8

Frank the Pirate's Wife's Chicken

1	large chicken
1 cup (250mL)	cornflake crumbs
2 Tbsp (25mL)	sesame seeds
2 Tbsp (25mL)	sunflower seeds
1 Tbsp (15mL)	rolled oats
1 tsp (5mL)	garlic powder
1 tsp (5mL)	ginger
1 tsp (5mL)	oregano
1 tsp (5mL)	tarragon
1 tsp (5mL)	saffron
1 tsp (5mL)	salt
	freshly ground pepper

Wash chicken thoroughly, dry with paper towels and cut into serving pieces. Do not remove skin. Grind remaining ingredients together in a blender then use to coat chicken.

Place chicken on a baking pan which has been covered with aluminum foil. Bake at 375°F (190°C) for 1 hour.

Serves 4

Dishwasher Salmon

4 pounds (2kg)	salmon (approx.)
¼ pound (125g)	butter, cut into small pieces
	salt and pepper
½ cup (125mL)	slivered almonds
1 cup (250mL)	white wine

Wash and dry salmon. Place on a large piece of heavy-duty aluminum foil. Dot fish inside and out with butter. Sprinkle with salt, pepper, and almonds. Douse with white wine.

Fold aluminum around fish, sealing perfectly. Wrap again in a second layer of foil and again seal perfectly.

Set on hottest and longest cycle of dishwasher which has a booster heat element. (Ordinary dishwashers will not produce sufficient heat to cook fish.) Run through 2 cycles. Salmon may also be cooked in the oven. Bake at 375°F (190°C) for 40 minutes.

Serves 6

Bruce Parsons, *Ripe and Raw,* 1972. Colour
photograph, 19.5 cm × 24.5 cm. Collection of the
artist.

Bruce Parsons

Toronto artist Bruce Parsons often spends summers leading workshops in the Maritimes, far from York University where he teaches. A strange thing happened in the summer of 1978, when Bruce was conducting a two-week art workshop on the environment at the St. Michael's Printshop in rural Newfoundland.

"While working with the twelve participants," says Bruce, "a chance suggestion added the sense of taste to the visual, descriptive, and tactile methods we were exploring for making contact with the natural surroundings.

"It happened by accident. Somebody brought in some cookies which triggered the suggestion and from there it took off. In a sense it turned into a two-week cookshop. Very exciting things happened to us, starting with catching the food and then with the things the participants did in preparing it. The whole thing was very much a function of the people in the group. Another set of people of course would not have acted and reacted in the same way.

"We got some of our cooking supplies from St. John's, but most of it came from our garden, the Atlantic coastline. From the sea we got crab, terns, capelin, sea urchins fresh from tidal pools, broken with a rock, their gonads eaten with the fingers, puffins, mussels that we steamed and dipped in garlic butter, winkles steamed and eaten with a pin, clams, cod, herring, squid, mackerel, scallops, lobster, and oysters. And the participants turned these into fantastic meals.

"We had chowders, *crab au gratin*, roast partridge, and baked mussels, a large salmon

baked in an egg sauce, lentil soup and a sunflower seed soup, lichee rice, herb bread, flageolet salad and lime fruit crumb pie."

The whole experience was very far removed from life in Toronto. "We really lived like kings for two weeks," Bruce says.

Warren Brownridge's Whole Wheat Herbed Sesame Bread

1 Tbsp (15mL)	sugar
2 cups (500mL)	lukewarm water
2 packages	yeast
1 Tbsp (15mL)	salt
2 Tbsp (25mL)	sugar
4 Tbsp (50mL)	vegetable oil
5 cups (1.25L)	flour (approx.), a mixture of whole wheat and white
1 tsp (5mL)	dried parsley
1 tsp (5mL)	oregano
1 tsp (5mL)	thyme
1 tsp (5mL)	garlic powder
1 tsp (5mL)	sage
2 tsp (10mL)	dry mustard
¼ tsp (1mL)	ginger
½ tsp (2mL)	dill seeds
	cornmeal
	sesame seeds
1	egg white, beaten with 1 tsp (5mL) water

Dissolve sugar in warm water. Add yeast. Set aside for 10 minutes. Stir in salt, sugar, and oil. Beat in 2 cups (500 mL) flour, mixing well, then gradually add remaining flour and herbs. When mixture becomes too stiff to stir, turn out onto floured board and knead in remaining flour until dough becomes smooth and elastic. Shape dough into a ball and place in a large buttered bowl, turning dough so all sides are buttered. Cover with a towel and set to rise in a warm, draft-free place until double in bulk—about 1 hour.

Punch dough down. Let rise again, covered, for about 1 hour.

Punch dough down again. Divide in 2 equal pieces. Roll out each piece to about 16 inches by 12 inches (40cm by 30cm). Roll up and pinch edges together.

Sprinkle a baking pan with cornmeal and sesame seeds. Place loaves on baking pan. Slash the top of each in 8 diagonal slices. Brush with egg white and water mixture. Sprinkle with sesame seeds. Cover with a towel and let rise for 1 hour. Bake at 425°F (220°C) for 10 minutes. Brush again with egg white mixture. Reduce heat to 350°F (180°C) and bake for a further 30 minutes or until bread sounds hollow when thumped on the bottom.

Yield: 2 loaves

Hanny Muggeridge's Sunflower Seed Soup

1 Tbsp (15mL)	butter
6	bacon strips, cut in small pieces
1	medium onion, finely chopped
4 cups (1L)	chicken stock
⅓ cup (75mL)	sunflower seed pieces

Melt butter. Add bacon and onion and sauté until golden. Pour off fat. Add chicken stock and sunflower seeds.

Simmer, covered, for 20 minutes. Ladle into heated soup bowls.

Serves 4

Dianne St. Croix's Clam Chowder

1 pound (500g)	clams (canned or steamed and removed from the shell)
2 cups (500mL)	diced potato
2	onions, finely chopped
¼ cup (50mL)	chopped parsley
¼ cup (50mL)	diced carrot
¼ tsp (1mL)	oregano
¼ tsp (1mL)	thyme
1 tsp (5mL)	salt
	freshly ground pepper
	water and/or milk

Combine all ingredients in a large saucepan. Cover with water or a mixture of half water and half milk. Cover and simmer for 30 minutes. This is best cooked beforehand and reheated.

Serves 4

Dianne St. Croix's Baked Clams or Mussels

6 dozen	clams or mussels
2 cups (500mL)	fresh bread crumbs
½ cup (125mL)	melted butter
1 tsp (5mL)	salt
	freshly ground pepper
¼ cup (50mL)	chopped parsley

Steam clams or mussels in a small amount of water for 5 minutes. Discard any that have not opened. Remove meat from shells, chop coarsely and combine with remaining ingredients. Fill half shells attractively.

Drizzle with more melted butter. Bake at 350°F (180°C) for 20 minutes or until heated through.

Yield: Approximately 2 dozen shells. Serves 6 as an appetizer

Dianne St. Croix's Pan-fried Sole or Flounder

1 pound (500g)	sole or flounder fillets
1	beaten egg
¼ cup (50mL)	flour
1 cup (250mL)	fine dry bread crumbs
1 Tbsp (15mL)	chopped parsley
1 tsp (5mL)	salt
¼ tsp (1mL)	basil
¼ tsp (1mL)	cayenne
¼ tsp (1mL)	garlic powder
	butter

Wash and dry fillets. Cut into triangular shapes.

Combine egg and flour. Set aside. Combine bread crumbs and herbs. Set aside.

Dip fish fillets first in egg mixture and then in bread crumb mixture.

Heat butter in a heavy frying pan. Fry fillets 5 minutes per side, turning only once.

Serves 4

Warren Brownridge's Lichee Rice

3 cups (750mL)	water or stock
1½ cups (375mL)	rice
1 tsp (5mL)	chopped parsley
1 tsp (5mL)	salt
½ tsp (2mL)	oregano
½ tsp (2mL)	basil
½ tsp (2mL)	dry mustard
½ tsp (2mL)	garlic powder
2 Tbsp (25mL)	butter
1	garlic clove, crushed
¼ cup (50mL)	finely diced onion
¼ cup (50mL)	finely diced celery
¼ cup (50mL)	finely diced green pepper
¼ cup (50mL)	finely diced carrot
1 20-ounce (567-g)	can lichee fruit, drained

Boil water or stock. Add rice, herbs, mustard, and garlic powder. Stir together. Cover and boil gently until rice is cooked and all liquid is absorbed—about 25 minutes.

Meanwhile, melt butter, add garlic clove, then sauté the diced vegetables.

Toss the rice with the sautéed vegetables. Turn into a heated serving dish and top with lichee fruit.

Serves 6

Andrée Laliberté-Bourge's Flageolet Salad

2 cups (500mL)	flageolets (dried baby lima beans)
¾ cup (175mL)	sliced hearts of palm
⅓ cup (75mL)	slivered almonds
8	black olives, sliced
½ cup (125mL)	olive oil
½ cup (125mL)	tarragon wine vinegar
1	garlic clove, crushed
1 tsp (5mL)	salt
	freshly ground pepper

Soak the beans overnight in water to cover. Boil until tender—about 1½ hours. Strain and cool.

Combine beans with remaining ingredients. Toss well. Cover with plastic wrap and chill for at least 1 hour before serving.

Serve on a bed of Romaine lettuce.

Serves 6

Warren Brownridge's Lime Fruit Crumb Pie

Pie Shell

1½ cups (375mL)	graham cracker crumbs
2 tsp (10mL)	cinnamon
pinch of	ginger
⅓ cup (75mL)	brown sugar
½ cup (125mL)	melted butter

Filling

2 cups (475mL)	milk
½ cup (125mL)	brown sugar
3 Tbsp (40mL)	flour
1 Tbsp (15mL)	cornstarch
pinch of	salt
3	beaten eggs
2 Tbsp (25mL)	butter
½ cup (125mL)	lime juice
	pitted cherries, strawberries, green grapes, blueberries, kiwi fruit, etc.
	toasted coconut and wheat germ

Combine pie shell ingredients and press firmly into bottom and sides of a 9-inch (1-L) pie plate. Chill for 1 hour.

Scald milk and set aside. In top of a double boiler, combine sugar, flour, cornstarch, and salt. Gradually add milk, stirring until thick. Stir a little of the hot milk mixture into the beaten eggs and then add all of the eggs to the milk mixture. Cook for 5 minutes, stirring constantly. Add butter and stir until melted. Remove from heat. Add lime juice.

Place a layer of sliced fruit in pie shell. Pour in half of the filling. Add another layer of sliced fruit and cover with remaining filling. Top with an attractive layer of fruit and sprinkle with coconut and wheat germ.

Fred Ross, *Still Life,* 1979. Mixed media, pastel, ink, and tempera, 91.4 cm × 73.7 cm. Private collection. Photo: Garey Pridham.

167

Christopher Pratt and Mary West Pratt

"I'm not a gourmet," says Newfoundlander Christopher Pratt, with a smile, "but my food habits have changed considerably since I imported a young New Brunswick girl to look after all my needs." The girl he "imported" is wife Mary West Pratt, who, in addition to being a noted painter (very frequently of food objects), has been taking good care of Christopher and their four children for some twenty-odd years.

"Mary makes a terrific health soup," says Chris, "which she says is a big cheat, but it's very nourishing and flavourful. It's so unlike the traditional Newfoundland way of making soup where you start boiling the turnips on Wednesday to eat the soup on Saturday!"

Somehow, Mary, who paints from eight in the morning until midnight most days, finds time to make interesting meals for the family. "I hurry to the kitchen at five to twelve to rush something to the table so everyone won't complain, and the soup recipe and others like it help. My daughters, Barbara and Ann, are both good cooks but they like especially to do things like breads and cakes. Kids always want to do the hard things, don't they, never the simple ones like tea biscuits."

"All our cooking is bounded by restrictions," she says. "No available fresh vegetables or fruit is the worst headache. We have to depend on frozen foods for the most part.

"But time is also a big problem. We really do like to eat nicely. We always set the table with proper placemats or a cloth. We usually use real table napkins although I resort to paper if I haven't time for ironing."

Like most Newfoundlanders, the Pratts cook a lot of fish. "As often as not, it's frozen, since it's much safer to buy it that way. I scale and gut it. I don't really know what all that stuff inside is. I have often cooked fish at the popular high heat temperature, but I really prefer to use a gentle heat and to stand around turning the creatures over and over until they flake easily and are nicely browned."

The St. Mary's Bay area where the Pratts live has a travelling beef salesman who comes around with his truck once a week. "He sells everything at $1.90 a pound, not differentiating between various cuts, so we usually get the tenderloin for that price. He seems to buy a cow on Wednesdays, which he then slaughters and hangs, and then he more or less cuts it to resemble proper beef cuts. Actually it sometimes looks as if it has been involved in a railway-crossing accident.

"I've learned a lot about different cooking in the years that I've lived here," says Mary. "During my first year as a Newfoundland bride, I gained forty pounds. We'd go to Christopher's parents' for Sunday dinners and be served chicken, roast beef, salt beef, turnip, cabbage and potatoes that had been cooked with the salt beef, and other vegetables cooked separately. To finish, we'd have two desserts—maybe spotted dick and partridge berry pudding with egg sauce. The choice was never between a hot or cold dessert, or a heavy or light one, there were just two desserts," remembers Mary.

"There was a maiden aunt living with my parents," explains Chris, "so there were two cooks in the house. Very often two things got made in case someone didn't like one of them."

Nowadays, Mary reads recipes for relaxation. "I have since I was a child. I used to curl up with cookbooks when all the other kids were reading manuals on things like how to catch a fish. But all this reading 'comes in' sometimes.

"We haven't always had enough money to eat extravagantly, but the restriction of money has been an interesting challenge and I think I was a better cook when I had to stretch the food we could afford.

"Having a solid New Brunswick understanding of basic cooking has been a great help. And having a mother who was careful about healthy food was a godsend."

Photo: John Reeves

Photo: John Reeves

Healthy Soup

1 10-ounce (284-mL)	can consommé diluted with 1 can water
1 14-ounce (398-mL)	can tomatoes
1 cup (250mL)	finely diced carrot
½ cup (125mL)	finely shredded cabbage
1	small onion, finely diced
½ cup (125mL)	finely diced celery
half a	green pepper, finely diced
1 14-ounce (398-mL)	can mushrooms, drained
1 tsp (5mL)	chili powder
1	bay leaf
dash of	Tabasco sauce

Combine all ingredients in a large saucepan. Simmer, covered, for 15 minutes, or until vegetables are cooked, but still crisp.

Serves 6

Mary's Chowder

3 large potatoes, peeled and thinly sliced
1 tsp (5mL) salt
1 Tbsp (15mL) butter
2 medium onions, diced
1 pound (500g) cod, cut in small pieces
½ cup (125mL) milk

Simmer sliced potatoes in just enough boiling salted water to cover until tender—about 15 minutes.

Meanwhile, heat butter in a heavy frying pan. Sauté onion until transparent. Add to the potatoes, along with the cod and milk. Simmer for a further 15 to 20 minutes or until cod flakes.

Serves 6

Cod with Savory Stuffing

1 4-pound (2-kg) cod
¼ cup (50mL) butter
1 onion, finely diced
2 cups (500mL) fresh bread crumbs
1 tsp (5mL) salt
freshly ground pepper
2 tsp (10mL) savory
3 thin strips salt pork

Remove head and tail from the cod. Wash thoroughly inside and out. Dry well.

Heat butter in a heavy frying pan. Add diced onion and sauté until limp. Combine with remaining ingredients except salt pork. Use to stuff fish cavity, then sew up opening using stiff thread.

Grease a clay baker or covered roasting pan. Place fish in baker. Cover with strips of salt pork. Bake covered at 350°F (180°C) for 1½ hours.

Serves 6

Fried Herring

6 herring
1 cup (250mL) flour
1 tsp (5mL) salt
freshly ground pepper
piece of salt pork

Wash herring and dry thoroughly with paper towels. Combine flour, salt, and pepper and coat fish well. Set aside for 20 minutes.

Place a heavy frying pan on low heat. Rub a piece of salt pork around the pan to grease it lightly.

Add herring. Fry over medium-low heat, turning frequently until fish flakes easily and is browned.

Serves 6

Trifle

1 pound cake
raspberry jam
2 12-ounce (340-g) packages frozen raspberries
2 14-ounce (398-mL) cans pears
¼ cup (50mL) sherry
1 package instant vanilla pudding
1 cup (250mL) whipping cream

Cut the pound cake in ½-inch (1-cm) slices. Make sandwiches of every two slices by filling with raspberry jam, then cut in "fingers." Put aside to "set."

Combine raspberries, pears, their juices, and sherry.

Make vanilla pudding according to package directions. Whip cream.

To assemble the trifle, line a large glass bowl with raspberry sandwich fingers. Pour in about 1 cup (250mL) of the fruit mixture and its juices. Top with a layer of pudding. Repeat process, alternating layers, continuing until all ingredients are used.

Top with whipped cream. Refrigerate for at least 4 hours before serving.

Serves 8

Mary West Pratt, *Red Currant Jelly,* 1976. Oil on
board, 44.5 cm × 44.5 cm. Collection of the National
Gallery of Canada, Ottawa.

Richard Prince

"I am anything but a gourmand," says Richard Prince, who is well known for his lively constructions. "I am probably one of the few people I know who will eat and even enjoy a Big Mac and will not complain about institutional food. However, I certainly enjoy a well-cooked meal eaten with pleasant company. To my way of thinking, the meal doesn't even have to be well cooked as long as the company is pleasant. Probably that is why we all have such fond memories of childhood birthday parties."

Even today, in the Prince family, whoever is celebrating a birthday gets to choose what he or she wants in the way of meals. Richard is likely to request pigs-in-blankets, toad-in-the-hole, and grasshopper pie.

Richard and Kathy Prince cook together in their Vancouver home, often trying out variations on favourite recipes—except for Richard's grasshopper pie, because, "There's no way to improve it."

"Generally, my taste in food runs along the meat-potato-vegetable track. We eat few desserts and in the summer turn to suitable fish and salads for the M-P-V routine. Breakfasts are an important meal with me, but the ones I eat are so appallingly distasteful to most people that I am reluctant to describe them."

Richard likes meat in the morning. The meat may turn up as frankfurters with cream of wheat or as an ingredient in his Doggie's Brekky—a pancake of leftovers that may include potatoes, cheese, meat, green onion, and eggs. He may also breakfast on his Garbage Compote Pie; this masterpiece results from a thorough fridge cleaning.

Photo: Michael Brodie

"You can probably tell that my approach to cooking is like my approach to art—eclectic.

"For me, eating has three functions. Firstly, it fills your stomach and if you haven't made it, you're not at liberty to complain about it even if you don't like it. Secondly, you have to eat because you have to fuel your body; and thirdly, eating is a social thing. I guess that's why we all do it."

Green Lump

½ pound (250g)	spinach egg noodles
2 Tbsp (25mL)	butter
half a	garlic clove, crushed
1 Tbsp (15mL)	milk
½ cup (125mL)	grated Cheddar cheese
1 Tbsp (15mL)	grated Parmesan cheese
3 Tbsp (40mL)	chopped green onion
1 Tbsp (15mL)	chopped parsley

Cook spinach noodles according to package directions. While they are cooking, make the sauce.

Melt butter in a heavy frying pan. Add garlic and sauté until golden. Stir in milk and cheese, letting the cheese melt. Add chopped green onion and heat through.

Drain noodles. Toss with sauce. Sprinkle with chopped parsley.

Serves 2

Improved Really Green Green Lump with the Wonderful Sauce

½ pound (250g)	frozen uncooked tortellini

Wonderful Sauce

3 Tbsp (40mL)	butter
2	garlic cloves, crushed
2 Tbsp (25mL)	chopped parsley
2 Tbsp (25mL)	chopped green onion
	salt and pepper
¼ tsp (1mL)	*fines herbes*
½ cup (125mL)	whipping cream
½ cup (125mL)	grated Parmesan cheese

Cook tortellini according to package instructions. While they are cooking, prepare the Wonderful Sauce.

Melt butter in a heavy frying pan. Add garlic, sauté until golden. Stir in parsley and green onion, salt, pepper, and *fines herbes*. Add whipping cream and cheese. Heat through but do not allow to boil.

Drain tortellini. Toss with sauce.

Serves 2

Baked Salmon

1 5-pound (2.5-kg)	salmon
1	small onion, sliced
1	lemon, sliced
½ tsp (2mL)	pepper
½ tsp (2mL)	basil
½ tsp (2mL)	*fines herbes*
6	whole green onions, stems included
3 Tbsp (40mL)	butter
2 Tbsp (25mL)	white wine

Wash and dry salmon. Fill cavity with sliced onion, half the lemon slices, pepper, basil, and *fines herbes*. Sew up cavity or fasten with skewers.

Place salmon on a large piece of heavy-duty aluminum foil. Put remaining lemon slices and green onions on top of fish. Dab with bits of butter. Pour on white wine. Fold aluminum foil together, sealing the edges completely. Bake at 325°F (160°C) for 1½ to 1¾ hours.

Serves 6 to 8

Salmon Spread

½ cup (125mL)	cooked salmon
½ cup (125mL)	cream cheese
1 Tbsp (15mL)	lemon juice or white vermouth
¼ tsp (1mL)	salt
	freshly ground pepper
¼ tsp (1mL)	*fines herbes*
1 tsp (5mL)	chopped parsley
2 tsp (10mL)	finely minced green onion

Combine all ingredients in a blender. Pureé until smooth. Spread on crackers or use as a dip.

Yield: 1 cup (250mL)

Richard's Chili con Carne

1 pound (500g)	ground beef
2	medium onions, finely chopped
1	green pepper, finely chopped
1	garlic clove, crushed
1 28-ounce (796-mL)	can red kidney beans
1 28-ounce (796-mL)	can tomatoes
1 tsp (5mL)	salt
	freshly ground pepper
2 Tbsp (25mL)	chili powder
2 Tbsp (25mL)	red wine vinegar
1	lemon, cut in tiny pieces, rind included

Brown meat in a heavy frying pan. Add onions, green pepper, and garlic. Stir until golden. Drain off all fat. Drain kidney beans and add to meat. Pour undrained tomatoes into blender. Purée for 10 seconds. Add to meat. Stir in salt, pepper, chili powder, vinegar, and lemon.

Simmer, covered, for 1 hour, stirring occasionally.

Serves 4

Mother's Gingersnap Cookies
The Best Cookies in the Western Hemisphere

1 cup (250mL)	molasses
1 cup (250mL)	shortening
1 cup (250mL)	brown sugar
4 cups (1L)	flour
1 tsp (5mL)	salt
1 tsp (5mL)	baking soda
4 tsp (20mL)	ginger

Bring molasses to the boil. Pour over shortening. Stir in brown sugar. Sift dry ingredients together. Combine with molasses mixture.

Divide dough in 4 pieces. Form each into a roll, 1½ inches (4cm) in diameter. Chill for several hours. Cut in thin slices less than ¼ inch (5mm) thick.

Place cookies on a greased baking pan. Bake at 350°F (180°C) for 6 to 8 minutes.

Yield: 10 dozen

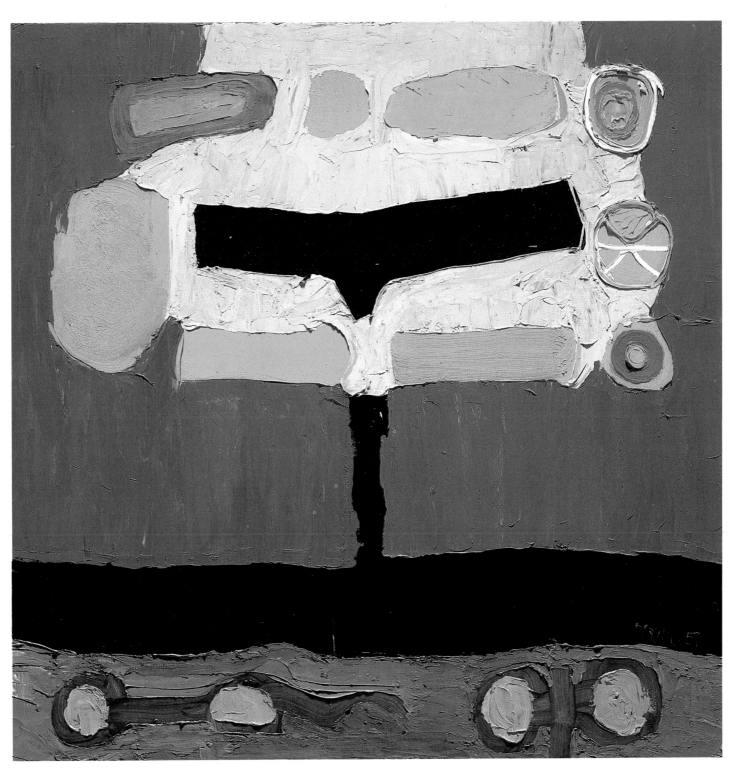

Harold Town, *Fruit Tree,* 1959. Oil on masonite,
91.4 cm × 91.4 cm. Collection of the artist. Photo:
VIDA/Saltmarche, Toronto.

Gordon Rayner

Gord Rayner lives in Toronto near his friends and colleagues Graham Coughtry and Robert Markle. They all like to eat a lot, frequently at each other's homes and studios, or together at favourite restaurants such as Casa Baldo.

"Graham and I used to go on painting trips together too, up along the Magnetewan River," Gord says. "We'd fish or shoot things like rabbit for our meals and have a good time preparing them. Once we wrote out a recipe for a rabbit stew we were preparing for dinner and we illustrated it with drawings starting with a picture of the gun barrel pointing at the rabbit.

"I like eating and I like asking in restaurants for recipes for things that I've enjoyed. Often I don't get them written down properly, though! At home I mostly improvise anyway or I'll refer to *The Joy of Cooking*."

Gord likes making soups. His French Onion is a favourite cold-weather soup and his Gazpacho is a frequently made summertime soup.

"It is said that in Spain there are as many variations of gazpacho as there are kitchens, each cook certain that his is the true one. After trying my recipe, you will, of course, realize that this is IT!"

Photo: VIDA/Saltmarche, Toronto

Gordon's Gazpacho

½ 10-ounce (284-mL)	can undiluted consommé
2 Tbsp (25mL)	white wine
1 Tbsp (15mL)	sherry
3 Tbsp (40mL)	lemon or lime juice
¼ cup (50mL)	olive oil
2	large tomatoes
1	garlic clove, crushed
1	Spanish onion, diced
1	stalk celery, diced
half a	green pepper, diced
half a	cucumber, seeds removed, diced
1 Tbsp (15mL)	chopped parsley
¼ tsp (1mL)	tarragon
¼ tsp (1mL)	salt
¼ tsp (1mL)	pepper
¼ tsp (1mL)	paprika
½ tsp (2mL)	basil
¼ tsp (1mL)	dry mustard
1 tsp (5mL)	Tabasco sauce
1 tsp (5mL)	Worcestershire sauce
1 Tbsp (15mL)	ketchup

Combine all ingredients in the container of a blender. Purée until smooth. Chill at least 6 hours before serving.

Accompany with cold beer or chilled white wine.

Serves 2

French Onion Soup for Two

3 Tbsp (40mL)	butter
1	Spanish onion, cut in thin slices
dash of	liquid Maggi seasoning
1 10-ounce (284-mL)	can consommé
2 Tbsp (25mL)	sherry
2 Tbsp (25mL)	red wine
pinch of	garlic powder
	salt and pepper
2	pieces rye or whole wheat bread
¼ cup (50mL)	grated cheese (any one or a combination of Gruyère, Cheddar, Parmesan or Mozzarella)
1 Tbsp (15mL)	chopped chives

Heat butter in heavy frying pan. Sauté onion until golden. Add a dash of liquid Maggi seasoning.

Heat consommé with an equal amount of water. Do not boil. Add sherry, wine, garlic powder, and salt and pepper to taste.

Heat 2 oven-proof soup bowls. Divide onions and consommé between them.

Cut bread slightly larger than circumference of bowls. Squeeze a slice into top of each bowl so that it is suspended above the soup and doesn't get soggy. Sprinkle with grated cheese and chives.

Bake at 350°F (180°C) for 20 minutes. Broil for 3 minutes to make the cheese crisp.

Serve with cold beer for hangovers or cold white wine for those sensuous Sunday brunches.

Serves 2

Don Reichert

Although Don and Mary Reichert's Winnipeg home and the adjoining studio come complete with a large garden and vegetable patch, they spend as much time as possible at their Bissett, Manitoba, house—a converted 1929 mine shed.

"We like outdoor living," explains Don, who can see the Red River out of his family-room window, "so we get away to Bissett as often as possible. It has a huge woodstove that doubles for cooking and heating, and we like to do a lot of our meals over an open fire."

Hunting and fishing provide the fare for many of their meals. They catch and cook venison, grouse, walleye, perch, and pike, among other things, and like the flavour of fish cooked in the same pan in which garlic sausage has been fried. "Or we cook country sausages on a stick over the fire.

"Very often, when a campfire is built, on granite outcroppings—abundant in pre-Cambrian shield country—pieces of rock will flake off the granite surface under the fire," says Don. "Whenever this happens, you should have a freshly caught panfish handy to take advantage of this beautiful and clean cooker-server. Simply turn the rock-dish over, exposing its clean underside, lay the fillets on this beautiful surface, turn them over when ready, and move away from the fire as the cooking proceeds, thereby allowing the rock to cool somewhat. There will be no difficulty eating the fish before it is overcooked or gets cold."

Don also has some expert advice to share on the matter of ruffled grouse.

"It is hard to do ruffled grouse or spruce hen justice away from a kitchen but they are very easy to clean and cook at a campfire. I can hear the groans now, but here is a method, assuming one has been recently obtained by some grisly means other than purchasing it at a supermarket.

"Grasp the bird by its feet, plant your own firmly on its wings and pull. The legs, viscera,

Photo: Michaelin McDermott

head, and skin will come away, leaving the breast and wings. The wings can be left on to protect the breast if it is to be carried with you for a while, or they can be removed and the breast cooked on a stick just like a piece of sausage, although perhaps with more care.

"Seems like a bold way to deal with a succulent morsel, but even with the minimum of salt and pepper, the meat is excellent though perhaps somewhat dry. Which reminds me that it would be nice to be with a friend who might just happen to have brought along a bottle of dry red wine or even a good sparkling rosé."

Huevos à la Mexicana

2 Tbsp (25mL)	bacon fat
1 tsp (5mL)	finely chopped onion
half a	ripe tomato, chopped
	finely chopped hot chili peppers to taste
2	eggs
2 Tbsp (25mL)	milk

Heat the bacon fat in a heavy frying pan. Sauté onion until limp. Add tomato and chili peppers.

Mix eggs and milk together using a fork. Pour into frying pan. Cook over medium heat, stirring, until eggs thicken.

Serves 1

Brown Buttery Sandwiches

butter
bread
suggested fillings: cooked meats
or poultry, sliced cheese,
pickles, peanut butter, sliced
onions, jam

Preheat a set of hinged sandwich irons over stove. Have at hand any favourite sandwich fillings. Spread filling between two slices of bread. Butter the outside of the bread. Enclose sandwich in irons, close, and trim off crusts. Return irons to heat. Cook until sandwich is brown on one side; then turn and brown the other side.

Roast Venison

1 4-pound (2-kg)	venison roast
½ cup (125mL)	water
6	bacon strips
1 cup (250mL)	tomato ketchup

Place meat on a rack in a shallow roasting pan. Pour in ½ cup (125mL) water. Place bacon strips across top of roast. Pour on ketchup and cover pan with a lid. Bake at 350°F (180°C) for 2 hours.

Serves 6 to 8

Corn Pudding

2 cups (500mL)	milk
1 7-ounce (199-mL)	can creamed corn
½ cup (125mL)	butter
1 cup (250mL)	cornmeal
2	eggs
1 tsp (5mL)	salt
½ tsp (2mL)	sugar
1 tsp (5mL)	baking powder

Scald milk and corn together. Set aside.

Melt butter. Stir in cornmeal. Heat until mixture bubbles.

Beat eggs. Add salt, sugar, and baking powder. Gradually stir in the hot milk mixture. Add to the cornmeal. Pour into a buttered 9-inch (2.5-L) cake pan. Bake at 350°F (180°C) for 30 to 40 minutes.

Bannock

3 cups (750mL)	flour
1 tsp (5mL)	baking powder
½ tsp (2mL)	salt
2 Tbsp (25mL)	lard
1¼ cups (300mL)	water (approx.)

Combine dry ingredients in a bowl. Cut in lard using a pastry blender or 2 knives. Make a well in the centre and pour in enough water to form a stiff but moist dough. Knead briefly. Pat into a flat shape, 12 inches (30cm) in diameter. Place in a lightly greased frying pan. Cook over medium heat for about 12 minutes per side, or until golden brown on the outside and cooked through.

Leslie Reid

"I may have twelve for dinner or I may be feeding only myself, but in either case, I like to make sure I cook really interesting things," says painter Leslie Reid, who lives in Ottawa.

"Mostly I shop in small stores. I dislike shopping in large supermarkets. I feel a great sense of alienation in them. I like to have a good stock of food on hand that I can put to use on the spur of the moment. It suits my style of cooking."

Leslie describes this style of cooking as "casual," with many of her favourite dishes being "derivative." She frequently uses an English cookbook by novelist Len Deighton but mostly seems to feel her way through recipes, intuitively putting together such complex things as osso bucco, ragouts, leeks provençal, ad hoc salad, trifles, and zabaglione, for instance. "They are different every time," she says.

Leslie has been exposed to varied cuisines all through her life. From her French-Canadian mother she learned an appreciation of those specialties, and having lived in England and France, where she studied painting for many years, she took advantage of the opportunities to learn about those cuisines.

"I'm always on to my friends to let me cook with them," she says. "It's an enjoyable activity and I like learning to do new things. And it's much more fun than cooking alone."

Photo: Renny Bartlett

Chicken and Ginger Ragout
(Thanks to Tak Tanabe)

1	chicken
2 Tbsp (25mL)	vegetable oil
2	onions, sliced
2	garlic cloves, crushed
3 Tbsp (40mL)	soy sauce
	juice of 1 lime
3	carrots, sliced thinly
2	zucchini, sliced thinly
1 Tbsp (15mL)	grated fresh ginger
½ 3-ounce (100-g)	package rice vermicelli soaked according to package directions
2 cups (500mL)	spinach leaves
1 cup (250mL)	chicken stock
	garnish of chopped green onion and grated fresh ginger

Wash and dry chicken. Cut into small serving pieces. Heat oil in a wok or heavy frying pan. Brown chicken pieces and cook for 15 to 20 minutes, stirring occasionally. Add onion and garlic. Sauté until golden. Add remaining ingredients except for the garnish. Cook, stirring, until spinach is wilted. Sprinkle with garnish.

Serves 4

Ratatouille

2 Tbsp (25mL)	vegetable oil
2 Tbsp (25mL)	butter
3	onions, chopped
4	garlic cloves, crushed
1 Tbsp (15mL)	brown sugar
4	red tomatoes, chopped
2	green tomatoes, chopped
1	eggplant, cubed
3	zucchini, sliced
2	green peppers, coarsely diced

Heat oil and butter in a heavy frying pan. Add onion and garlic. Sauté until golden. Add brown sugar. Stir in remaining ingredients. Cover and simmer for 15 minutes, stirring occasionally.

Serves 8

Gâteau Rothschild

⅔ cup (175mL)	dry bread crumbs
⅔ cup (175mL)	grated Parmesan cheese
½ cup (125mL)	chopped parsley
1 tsp (5mL)	salt
	freshly ground pepper
2 Tbsp (25mL)	vegetable oil
2 Tbsp (25mL)	butter
3	onions, sliced
½ pound (250g)	mushrooms, sliced
2	large red peppers, cut in rings
1	eggplant, sliced
6	tomatoes, sliced

Combine bread crumbs, cheese, parsley, salt, and pepper. Set aside.

Heat oil and butter in a heavy frying pan. Sauté onion slices until golden. Spoon into buttered baking dish. Sprinkle with a little of the cheese mixture. Sauté mushrooms in the same frying pan until brown and spoon over onions in baking dish. Sprinkle with cheese mixture. Add more oil and butter to frying pan if necessary and cook pepper, eggplant, and tomatoes, separately, layering each in the baking dish with a sprinkling of the cheese mixture. Finish with a layer of cheese. Bake at 350°F (180°C) for 15 to 20 minutes.

Serves 8

Granola (Thanks to Hilda Paz)

3 pounds (1.5kg)	rolled oats
2 cups (500mL)	coconut
2 cups (500mL)	sesame seeds
2 cups (500mL)	sunflower seeds
2 cups (500mL)	almonds
2 cups (500mL)	walnuts
2 cups (500mL)	soy oil
½ pound (250g)	honey
½ pound (250g)	raisins
1 pound (500g)	chopped dates

Combine all ingredients except raisins and dates. Mix together thoroughly.

Bake at 250°F (120°C) for 2 hours, stirring every half hour. When cool, add raisins and dates.

Yield: 4½ quarts (4.5L)

Alan Reynolds

Al Reynolds once traded a piece of his sculpture for a recipe, which tells a lot about the importance food has for him.

"When I was a student, I could afford to eat only once a week and it was then I made up my mind I'd never be hungry again."

As a result, Al pours the same intense effort into cooking as he does into an art work. "They're both creative experiences," he says.

From his famous New Year's Eve parties for thirty to his frequent fishing trips with friend and colleague Bruce O'Neil, Al puts a lot of thought and preparation into the foods that will be served on these occasions.

He counts on three cases of champagne to accompany the New Year's Eve buffet of Chicken Vinaigrette, curried fruit, a rice pilaf, and the grand finale, poppy seed cake, the recipe for which he traded the sculpture.

On a recent, typical fishing trip south of Edmonton, where he lives, he packed the hamper with boneless chicken breasts, tenderloin steaks, and bacon. "Bruce brought the beer so we had great meals. It didn't matter whether or not we caught any fish because we weren't depending on them."

Chicken Vinaigrette
(Stolen unashamedly from Marissa Wohllebe)

1	chicken
1	onion, studded with cloves
1	carrot, coarsely chopped
1	celery stalk
1	bay leaf
1 tsp (5mL)	salt
3 quarts (3L)	water

Sauce

4 tsp (20mL)	wine vinegar
1 cup (250mL)	olive oil
½ cup (125mL)	chopped parsley
1 Tbsp (15mL)	chopped chives
1 Tbsp (15mL)	chopped capers
1 Tbsp (15mL)	chopped green onion
1 Tbsp (15mL)	chopped sour pickle
½ tsp (2mL)	dry mustard
2	hard-boiled eggs, finely chopped
2 tsp (10mL)	salt
	freshly ground pepper

Bring chicken and remaining ingredients to a boil. Cover and simmer for 1 hour. Lift chicken from the stock. Cool.

Remove skin, separate meat from the bones and place meat on serving dish.

To prepare the sauce, combine all sauce ingredients and set aside to allow flavours to mingle for several hours before using.

To serve, pour sauce over chicken pieces.

Serves 4

Smoked Salmon Hollandaise

2 pounds (1kg)	smoked salmon, cut in strips ¼ inch (1cm) thick
4	small zucchini, sliced
2 dozen	mushrooms, sliced
2 cups (500mL)	Hollandaise Sauce
¼ cup (50mL)	chopped parsley
1	lemon, cut in wedges, as garnish

Lightly butter a shallow oven-to-table dish. Alternate rows of smoked salmon and sliced zucchini and sliced mushrooms in it. Cover with Hollandaise Sauce. Sprinkle with parsley. Bake at 350°F (180°C) for 20 to 25 minutes. Decorate with lemon wedges.

Serve with white rice and chilled white wine.

Serves 4

Hollandaise Sauce

1 cup (250mL)	cold butter
4	egg yolks, beaten
4 tsp (20mL)	fresh lemon juice
½ tsp (5mL)	salt
pinch of	cayenne

Place a small heavy enamel saucepan in the freezer to chill for 15 minutes. When ready to make sauce, place all ingredients in it set over low heat. With a spoon, gently rotate the cold butter around the saucepan until it has melted and the sauce has thickened.

Yield: 2 cups

Geoffrey Rock

"I'm an on-and-off cook," says Vancouver artist Geoffrey Rock. "I cook when I have time off from painting, but painting comes first. I find cooking to be very expressive, and while I enjoy making several things, I think I put most of my creative energies into Chili con Carne. Everybody likes it and it's always a big hit at parties. It's good for groups of ten or twelve people."

Geoffrey and Joan Rock have been married for thirty-eight years and Geoffrey calls his wife a marvellous cook. "I must admit though, that I sometimes get a bit tired of salads which Joan seems to make every day."

Having grown up in England, Geoffrey fondly remembers some of the foods he ate in his youth that he no longer gets in Canada. "I miss my roast pork with crackling that I had as a child in Birmingham. We never have that sort of thing here. Nonetheless, we still eat very well."

A talent for food seems to run in the family. One of the Rocks' sons is a chef in a Victoria restaurant. "And a terrific cook he is, too," says his father. "He probably inherited the talent!"

Chili con Carne

2 Tbsp (25mL)	butter
2	large onions, diced
2	garlic cloves, crushed
1 pound (500g)	lean ground beef
1 14-ounce (398-mL)	can tomatoes
1 14-ounce (398-mL)	can red kidney beans
1	green pepper, diced
half a	bottle ale
½ tsp (2mL)	celery seed
¼ tsp (1mL)	cayenne
1 tsp (5mL)	cumin seed, crushed
2	bay leaves
2 Tbsp (25mL)	chili powder
¼ tsp (1mL)	basil
¼ tsp (1mL)	oregano
dash of	soy sauce
	salt and pepper

Heat butter in a heavy frying pan. Add onion and garlic, and sauté until golden. Stir in meat and cook until brown. Pour off excess fat.

Strain tomatoes and add them to the frying pan. Stir in remaining ingredients except salt and pepper. Bring to the boil. Reduce heat and simmer gently, uncovered, for about 2 hours, or until thick, stirring occasionally. Taste for seasoning and add salt and pepper.

Serves 4

Steak au Poivre

4	club or filet mignon steaks
2 Tbsp (25mL)	coarsely ground black pepper
1 Tbsp (15mL)	butter
	salt
2 Tbsp (25mL)	chopped shallots or green onions
½ cup (125mL)	beef stock
2 Tbsp (25mL)	cognac
3 Tbsp (40mL)	soft butter
	parsley or watercress for garnish

Pat the steaks dry using paper towels. Sprinkle both sides of each steak with pepper, pressing it well into the meat with the heel of the hands. Cover with waxed paper and let stand for at least 1 hour.

Heat butter in a heavy frying pan. Sauté the steaks over high heat for 3 or 4 minutes on each side. Remove to a hot platter. Season with salt. Keep warm while preparing the sauce.

Pour most of the fat out of the frying pan. Add the shallots or green onions. Cook over low heat for 1 minute. Add the stock and over high heat, boil down rapidly for 1 minute. Stir in the cognac and continue to boil for a further 1 minute.

Turn off the heat and swirl in the soft butter a teaspoon at a time.

To serve, pour the sauce over the steaks and garnish with parsley or watercress.

Serves 4

Liver Creole

6	slices bacon, cut in small pieces
2	large onions, sliced into rings
1	garlic clove, crushed
1 pound (500g)	pork or beef liver, cut into bite-sized pieces
	flour
1 14-ounce (398-mL)	can tomatoes
½ tsp (2mL)	soy sauce
½ tsp (2mL)	Worcestershire sauce
½ cup (125mL)	diced celery
1	green pepper, sliced thinly
1	bay leaf
½ tsp (2mL)	salt
¼ tsp (1mL)	pepper

In a heavy frying pan sauté bacon, onions, and crushed garlic until golden brown.

Dredge liver pieces with flour, shaking to remove excess. Add to frying pan. Brown on all sides. Add remaining ingredients. Simmer, covered, for 1 hour.

Serve accompanied by green vegetables and mashed potatoes.

Serves 4

William Ronald

"When I was both painting and doing a lot of media work, we started having champagne breakfasts in order to see people," says Toronto painter William Ronald. "It was a great way to get the day going.

"One of my fantasies is to imagine a whole day spent eating. I have the menu in mind; it looks like this:

Breakfast
Honeydew melon with prosciutto ham
Gamblers' eggs
Baked back bacon
Croissants
Strawberries in kirsch
Coffee
Champagne

Lunch
Onion soup
Marinated flank steak served on French or Italian bread
California salad
Pineapple whip
Coffee or tea
Red wine

Dinner
Shrimp cocktail
Veal scallops in white wine
Buttered noodles with crumbs
Fresh asparagus with Hollandaise sauce
Caesar salad
Peach flambé
White wine
Coffee or tea

Late-night snack
Caviar on toast
Crab-devilled eggs
Napoleon brandy

It's all very Bacchanalian and very sexy, and of course, you could never make it through a day having eaten all this, but I still like to imagine it."

Photo: William Glenesk

Veal Scallops in White Wine

2 pounds (1kg)	veal scallops, very thinly sliced
½ cup (125mL)	flour
4 Tbsp (50mL)	butter
⅔ cup (175mL)	dry white wine
½ tsp (2mL)	salt
	freshly ground pepper
1 cup (250mL)	beef stock
1 Tbsp (15mL)	chopped parsley, as garnish

Pat scallop slices dry with a paper towel. Dredge with flour. Melt butter in a heavy frying pan. Sauté veal, a few pieces at a time, until lightly browned. Keep warm while browning remaining slices. Stir wine into pan. Scrape brown bits from bottom and sides. Add salt, pepper, and stock. Simmer for 2 minutes. Return veal to pan. Cover and simmer for 5 minutes.

Serve garnished with chopped parsley.

Serves 6

Flank Steak

1	large flank steak
½ cup (125mL)	sherry
½ cup (125mL)	soy sauce
½ cup (125mL)	olive oil
½ cup (125mL)	grated onion
1	garlic clove, crushed
½ tsp (2mL)	grated fresh ginger root
1 Tbsp (15mL)	chopped parsley

Marinate steak in remaining ingredients for 3 hours, turning occasionally.

Broil 5 minutes per side, 4 inches (10cm) from heat. Slice diagonally, paper thin.

Serve on slices of hot Italian bread.

Serves 6

California Salad

3	large tomatoes
1	large onion
1	green pepper
½ tsp (2mL)	salt
½ tsp (2mL)	dry mustard
¼ tsp (1mL)	celery seed
2 Tbsp (25mL)	vinegar

Cut tomatoes, onion, and green pepper into very thin slices. Cover with seasonings and vinegar. Let marinate for several hours or overnight.

Serves 6

Gamblers' Eggs

Pile scrambled eggs on toasted French bread and cover with hot tomato sauce.

Pineapple Whip

1 14-ounce (398-mL)	can crushed pineapple
16	marshmallows, cut in quarters
1 cup (250mL)	whipping cream
1 tsp (5mL)	vanilla
2 tsp (10mL)	confectioners sugar

Combine pineapple and marshmallows. Cover and refrigerate for 1 hour. Drain. Whip the cream, adding vanilla and sugar. Fold into pineapple and marshmallow mixture.

Serves 4

Fred Ross

"Living in the Maritimes means that our eating habits are to a great extent determined by our proximity to the sea," says Fred Ross. "In the summer months when we're at our place in St. Andrew's, we haunt Robichaud's Fish Market for many of our meals, buying such things as halibut, salmon, lobster, and, of course, scallops. Sheila does wonderful things with all of them."

"We eat very much according to the seasons," says Sheila Ross, who teaches ballet in Saint John. "In the summers, we have all the fresh things from our vegetable garden, including a variety of herbs."

"We tend to eat healthy foods, and almost never touch cakes or pastries, although Sheila makes a delicious apple crisp with wheat germ," Fred adds.

"In the mornings when the kids are in a rush to get off for school, we'll put some yoghurt, pineapple juice, and orange juice in the blender and buzz it up. It seems like a good way to start the day."

"Fred would never tell you this," says Sheila, "but he makes wonderful sandwiches." The Rosses like dense whole wheat bread; Sheila bakes it and Fred makes the sandwiches. "I don't know what makes them so good," says Sheila, "but perhaps it's because he doesn't squish them together. Everyone always eats far more than they should when Fred has made them!"

Zucchini Stuffed with Veal

2	large zucchini
2 Tbsp (25mL)	safflower oil
2	onions, chopped
1	garlic clove, crushed
1 pound (500g)	boneless veal, cut in bite-sized pieces
½ 14-ounce (398-mL)	can tomatoes
2 dozen	small mushrooms
1 Tbsp (15mL)	chopped parsley
1 tsp (5mL)	marjoram
2 tsp (10mL)	lemon juice
1 tsp (5mL)	salt
	freshly ground pepper
½ cup (125mL)	grated Parmesan cheese

Blanch zucchini in boiling salted water for 10 minutes and drain. Cut in half lengthwise and scoop out a bit of the flesh to make a hollow.

Heat oil in a heavy frying pan. Sauté onion and garlic until golden. Remove from pan. Add cubed veal to remaining oil. Sauté until brown. Return onions and garlic to pan. Add remaining ingredients except for the Parmesan cheese. Simmer, covered, for 10 minutes.

Spoon meat mixture into zucchini halves. Sprinkle with Parmesan cheese. Bake at 350°F (180°C) for 45 minutes. Just before serving, sprinkle with a little more cheese and broil to crisp it.

Serves 4

Apple Crisp

¾ cup (175mL)	flour
¾ cup (175mL)	wheat germ
1 cup (250mL)	brown sugar
	grated rind of 1 lemon
1 tsp (5mL)	cinnamon
pinch of	salt
½ cup (125mL)	butter
2 cups (500mL)	tart apples, sliced
	cinnamon

Combine dry ingredients. Cut in butter using a pastry blender or 2 knives. Set aside.

Butter a 9-inch (2.5-L) square cake pan. Spread sliced apples over the bottom. Sprinkle with cinnamon.

Cover with crumbly mixture, pressing it down firmly. Bake at 350°F (180°C) for 35 minutes.

Serve warm with whipped cream or yoghurt.

Whole Wheat Bread

½ cup (125mL)	lukewarm water
1 tsp (5mL)	sugar
1 package	yeast
3 Tbsp (40mL)	butter
2 Tbsp (25mL)	sugar
1 Tbsp (15mL)	salt
1 cup (250mL)	boiling water
1 cup (250mL)	milk
2½ cups (625mL)	whole wheat flour
2½ cups (625mL)	white flour

Combine lukewarm water, sugar and yeast in a large bowl. Let stand for 10 minutes.

Combine butter, sugar, salt, and boiling water in another bowl. Stir to melt butter. Allow mixture to cool, then add milk. Combine with yeast. Stir in whole wheat flour, beating well. Gradually add white flour. When dough becomes too stiff to beat, turn out onto a floured board and knead in remaining flour until dough is smooth and elastic.

Form dough into a ball. Place in a greased bowl and turn so all sides are greased. Cover with a towel and let rise in a warm, draft-free place until double in bulk—about 1 hour.

Punch dough down. Divide in 2 pieces. Knead each piece briefly. Form into 2 loaves and place in greased bread pans. Cover with a towel and let rise until double in bulk.

Bake at 400°F (200°C) for 40 minutes. Remove from pans and rub sides and tops with butter to give a shiny crust.

Yield: 2 loaves

Michael Snow and Joyce Wieland

In Michael Snow and Joyce Wieland's house there is a sharing of kitchen duties, although Joyce is very much in charge. "I usually do the cooking and Michael does the dishes," she says. "He gets a better meal that way!

"Our house in Toronto is very small so we don't entertain very often and then no more than four people at a time. Maybe I'm lazy."

Joyce and Michael are very aware of nutrition. "We take supplementary organic vitamins and drink only bottled water," says Michael. "Joyce knew about health foods and was concerned about ecology long before it became a fad."

It may all have started many years ago, when Michael's mother persuaded them to add lecithin to sauces instead of fats. It was she who sparked Joyce's interest in the history of foods and food habits. "I'm doing a lot of research into old foods and the ways the ancients and pioneers foraged," Joyce says. "Ourselves, we gather wild foods when we go to our cabin in northern Quebec and there we cook everything on a woodstove so I have some feeling for this."

Originally from Chicoutimi, Michael's mother is an excellent cook, particularly of regional dishes. Joyce uses her large volume of hand-written recipes, which has been compiled by several generations of her family.

"I think there are a lot of different cuisines nowadays that are getting mixed in with the established cuisines and producing new results," says Joyce. "My next project is to learn how to preserve things by some new means of technology, but I don't know yet what it is."

Karch Chicken, Soup and Sauce

	1	chicken
	3	onions
	3	parsnips, sliced
	1	bay leaf
2 quarts (2L)		water
	8	chicken-stock cubes
	8	carrots, sliced in half
	5	potatoes, cut in chunks
½ cup (125mL)		chopped parsley
¼ pound (125g)		fine soup noodles

Sauce

1 cup (250mL)	yoghurt
2 Tbsp (25mL)	horseradish
1 tsp (5mL)	honey

Combine chicken, onions, parsnips, bay leaf, water, and stock cubes. Bring to the boil. Reduce heat and simmer, covered, for 20 minutes. Add carrots and potatoes and simmer for a further hour.

Remove chicken to a platter and surround with vegetables. Keep warm.

Boil soup noodles in a separate pot according to package directions. Skim fat from chicken stock. Stir in parsley.

Spoon noodles into each soup bowl. Top with soup.

Combine sauce ingredients. Carve chicken and serve with accompanying vegetables and sauce.

Serves 6

Fermented Oatcakes

2 cups (500mL)	oats (from health-food store)
1½ cups (375mL)	buttermilk
1 cup (250mL)	flour
1 tsp (5mL)	baking soda

Combine oats and buttermilk. Let stand, covered, at room temperature for 2 days. Add flour and baking soda. Pat to ½-inch (1-cm) thickness. Cut into 2-inch (5-cm) circles. Grease a heavy frying pan lightly. Cook oatcakes over medium heat for 10 minutes per side.

Yield: 15 cakes

Auntie Imperialist Cakes

An Unselfish People

Wherever and whenever Canadians have made revolution, they have always sat around the campfire and made these little cakes and listened to fiddle music. An unselfish people, they usually give away everything, especially to the Americans. In their great simplicity, their greatest pleasure comes from sitting on the ground eating these little symbols of what's left. This is how the term leftover came into use.

J. Wieland, 1974

½ cup (125mL)	wheat germ
1 cup (250mL)	buckwheat flour
1 Tbsp (15mL)	safflower oil
1 Tbsp (15mL)	baking soda
2	fertile eggs
1½ cups (375mL)	buttermilk
1 cup (250mL)	thinly sliced fresh strawberries, raspberries, blueberries, or currants

Combine all ingredients into a thin batter.

Lightly oil a heavy frying pan. Pour in a large spoonful of batter so that each pancake spreads to no more than 3 inches (7cm) in diameter. Cook until brown on the underside, then turn over and cook lightly until brown on the other side.

May be eaten hot or cold.

Yield: 36 cakes

Gerald Squires

Thirty miles south of St. John's on the east coast of Newfoundland is the tiny town of Ferryland. Jutting a couple of miles out into the sea is a steep, skinny peninsula at the end of which perches the Ferryland lighthouse. And for the past dozen years, Gerry and Gail Squires and their two teenaged children have lived in that lighthouse.

"It's automated," they explain, "but if anything goes wrong, we have to report it."

Needless to say, the view is spectacular—not only of the pounding waves of the sea, the craggy shoreline, and the timbered terrain, but also of the wildlife and sea creatures that live nearby and provide the Squires with food.

"We live pretty cheaply off the land and sea," explains Gerry, who paints in a nearby studio. "It's all free—the wild birds, the terns and puffins, plus the capelin, cod, mackerel, salmon, lobster, crab, and squid, and other fish, and the moose, caribou, and rabbits from the land. I could go out and jig and in one autumn day, catch enough fish to last us through the winter."

As is typical with most rural Newfoundlanders, the Squires grow most of their own vegetables too, wintering them in a root cellar.

"We can almost always feed a small army on short notice," says Gail. "Once we had a CBC film crew here so I boiled a washtub full of Jigs Dinner. Forty pounds of salt meat went into it. You can understand why this is the basic dinner of the province because so many Newfoundlanders have such large families.

"We bake all our own bread, too," says Gail. "Even the kids do it. So much of the cooking in our house is varied according to what's available that it's hard to say how anything will turn out. It makes giving recipes very difficult!"

"We like getting together with friends, all of us taking along food for a picnic feast

Photo: Robin MacKenzie

somewhere," says Gerry. "And then I remember the time that everything around here got curried because a young Indian by the name of Malachai Singh wandered into town and claimed to be a cook. He got hired somewhere and soon we found ourselves eating curried moose and curried cod tongues and curried lots of things that had never before been curried.

"We're really very much interested in all sorts of food. Cooking and art are very similar in that you work with what you have, and in that both can either be spontaneous actions or very contrived."

Newfoundland-style Bread

1 Tbsp (15mL)	sugar
2 packages	yeast
1 cup (250mL)	lukewarm water
5 pounds (2.5kg)	white flour
2 pounds (1kg)	whole wheat flour
1 cup (250mL)	toasted sesame seeds
1 cup (250mL)	soy grits
3 Tbsp (40mL)	salt
2 cups (500mL)	Red River cereal
1 cup (250mL)	molasses
2 quarts (2L)	warm water (approx.)

Combine sugar, yeast, and water. Set aside for 10 minutes.

Combine flours, sesame seeds, soy grits, salt, and cereal in a very large bowl. Gradually stir in molasses, water, and yeast mixture, using hands if necessary. Knead dough until smooth and elastic—about 15 minutes. Form into a ball and set in a greased bowl, turning so all sides are greased. Cover with a towel and let rise in a warm, draft-free place until double in bulk.

Punch dough down and let rise again until double in bulk. Divide into 7 pieces. Shape into loaves and place in greased loaf pans. Cover with towels and let rise until dough is about 1 inch (2.5cm) above the rim of the pans.

Bake at 350°F (180°C) for 1 hour. Remove from pans and cool on wire racks.

Yield: 7 loaves

Garam Masala

1 cup (250mL)	coriander seeds
½ cup (125mL)	cumin seeds
¼ cup (50mL)	black peppercorns
1	cinnamon stick, broken in pieces
2 Tbsp (25mL)	white cardamom seeds, shells removed and discarded
3	bay leaves

Put all ingredients in a blender. Cover and grind into a fine powder.

Yield: 1½ cups (375mL)

Curried Cod Tongues à la Malachai Singh

2 pounds (1kg)	fresh or frozen cod tongues
¼ pound (125g)	salt pork, finely diced
¼ cup (50mL)	flour
2 tsp (10mL)	garam masala or curry powder
1 tsp (5mL)	salt
	freshly ground pepper
sprinkling of	cayenne
2 tsp (10mL)	finely grated lemon rind

Wash tongues and dry thoroughly. Sauté diced salt pork in a heavy frying pan until crisp. Remove pieces with a slotted spoon and set aside on paper towels. Use remaining fat to fry tongues. Fat should be ½ inch (1cm) deep. Add oil if necessary.

Mix together flour, garam masala, salt, pepper, and cayenne in a bag. Shake cod tongues in it.

Heat fat until sizzling hot. Fry tongues, uncovered, until crusty brown, turning only once—about 8 to 10 minutes per side. They should be firm yet juicy.

To serve, sprinkle with grated lemon rind and reserved salt pork.

Serves 6

Capelin

5	small fresh capelin per person
	flour
	clarified butter or pork fat

Remove the heads just behind the gills. Slit open along the belly and clean out with a finger or knife. Wash well under running cold water and dry thoroughly.

Roll in flour and fry in clarified butter or pork fat about 3 minutes per side. The fish is cooked when the flesh flakes easily and is pearly white.

Capelin may also be broiled. Brush both sides of each fish with melted butter before putting under the broiler.

Serve with sour cream or lemon-caper butter.

Curried Moose

1 pound (500g)	lean moose meat
2 Tbsp (25mL)	vegetable oil
2 Tbsp (25mL)	butter
2	onions, chopped
4	garlic cloves, crushed
1 Tbsp (15mL)	grated fresh ginger root
1 tsp (5mL)	turmeric
2 tsp (10mL)	salt
2 tsp (10mL)	garam masala (see page 193) or curry powder
½ tsp (2mL)	cayenne
3	tomatoes, sliced
1	green pepper, diced
1½ cups (375mL)	water

Cut meat into bite-sized pieces. Set aside.

Heat oil and butter in a heavy frying pan. Add onion, garlic, and ginger root and sauté until limp. Stir in turmeric, salt, garam masala, and cayenne. Combine well. Add moose meat and sauté until brown. Cover and simmer over low heat for about 35 minutes.

Add sliced tomatoes, green pepper, and water. Bring to the boil, reduce heat, and simmer for another 35 minutes. If too much liquid remains, remove lid and boil for a few minutes to evaporate it.

Serve with rice or chapaties, garnished with chopped parsley.

Serves 4

Jigs Dinner with Peas Pudding and Dough Boys

2 pounds (1kg)	salt beef
2 cups (500mL)	split peas
1	cabbage, cut in chunks
2	turnips, cubed
2	onions, quartered
6	carrots, cut in chunks
3	potatoes, cubed
1 cup (250mL)	flour
2 tsp (10mL)	baking powder
¾ cup (175mL)	milk

Soak salt beef overnight, covered with water. In a separate pot, soak split peas overnight covered with water. The next day, drain both.

Put the meat in a large pot. Cover with water. Tie up the peas in a clean cloth bag. Lower it into the pot with the meat. Bring to the boil. Reduce heat and simmer, covered, for 3 hours. Remove bag of peas and reserve. Add cabbage, turnips, onions, carrots, and potatoes to the pot. Cover and simmer for 30 minutes, then return bag of peas to the pot.

Make dough boys by combining flour and baking powder in a bowl and adding enough milk to make a stiff dough. Drop by the spoonful into the pot of meat and vegetables. Cover and cook for 15 minutes.

Remove peas pudding. Turn it out of the bag and mash with butter and pepper.

Serve meat and vegetables with peas pudding on the side and dough boys on top.

Serves 8

Carol Sutton and André Fauteux

In spite of widely differing backgrounds (he is a sculptor from Quebec and she a painter from Virginia), Carol Sutton and André Fauteux find they enjoy eating the same kinds of foods and cooking them together. "We share kitchen duties equally, which is possible because we're very much equals in terms of interest and expertise too," says Carol.

"But when André was a child," she continues, "his family ate a lot of canned foods. On the other hand, my parents were phenomenal gourmets—they must have had a collection of over a thousand cookbooks and they were forever entertaining and doing all the preparations together. Occasionally we children were allowed to help get things ready for dinner parties or whatever."

Such early exposure and training appear to be responsible for Carol's passion for food today, but it's a passion that demands excellence. Pots of healthy herbs grow on the deep window sills of their Toronto home and they try to use fresh ingredients wherever possible. "If we have to substitute and use something frozen, I'll scout around until I find the best brand. They're not all equally good, you know."

Carol and André are determined about perfecting certain recipes. "Coming from Virginia, I love spoonbread," Carol says, "but I must have tried twenty different recipes before I found one I was satisfied with.

"We were in Rome once and had a superb spaghetti dish made with Pancetta salami. When we got home, we experimented several times until we figured we had duplicated it pretty closely."

Getting a food processor expanded their culinary horizons considerably. "It's such a timesaver and helps one get organized," they say.

"It extends your possibilities fantastically. I'll get everything ready for dinner before I leave for the studio in the morning," says Carol, "usually using my Cuisinart. It's such a treat not to come home to boggy stews anymore."

Like her parents, Carol and André have a large cookbook collection. "I really like the *Colonial Williamsburg Cookbook* because there are so many good southern recipes in it, and another of my favourites is Perla Meyers' *The Seasonal Kitchen* because her approach and philosophy are similar to mine," says Carol. "And since we got our Cuisinart, I'm devoted to Roy Andries de Groot's *Cooking with the Cuisinart*."

Spaghetti Pancetta

2 Tbsp (25mL)	olive oil
½ pound (250g)	pancetta, skin removed and cut in ½-inch (1-cm) cubes
1	onion, finely chopped
	freshly ground pepper
1 pound (500g)	spaghetti noodles
2	eggs
½ cup (125mL)	grated Parmesan cheese

Heat oil in a heavy frying pan. Sauté diced pancetta until it is quite crisp. Add onion. Stir until golden. Drain off fat until no more than 1 tablespoon (15mL) remains. Grind pepper over pancetta mixture and keep warm.

Meanwhile, cook spaghetti according to package directions and drain well.

Crack eggs in a large bowl that has been slightly warmed. Beat with a wire whisk until they begin to froth. Add a bit more freshly ground pepper. Pour in the cooked, drained spaghetti. Toss well until the heat from the spaghetti has cooked the eggs and the pasta is evenly coated. Add pancetta mixture and Parmesan cheese and toss.

Serves 4

Carol's Best-Ever Fresh in Season Spaghetti

1½ pounds (750g)	ground beef
1 tsp (5mL)	oregano
1 tsp (5mL)	basil
½ tsp (2mL)	*herbes de Provence*
2 Tbsp (25mL)	Worcestershire sauce
2	small onions
1	large Spanish onion
1	bunch green onions, stems included
3	stalks celery, leaves included
15	pimento-stuffed olives
20	large fresh Italian plum tomatoes
½ cup (125mL)	olive-packing juice
1 4-ounce (100-mL)	can tomato paste
5	sprigs fresh basil
6	sprigs fresh parsley
6	garlic cloves
	freshly ground pepper
2 pounds (1kg)	vermicelli noodles, cooked

Brown beef in a heavy frying pan. Add oregano, basil, *herbes de Provence* and Worcestershire sauce. Transfer to a heavy casserole. In a food processor or with a knife, chop the onions, celery, and olives. Sauté until limp in 2 tablespoons (25mL) of the fat remaining in the frying pan. Combine with meat in the casserole.

Combine plum tomatoes and remaining ingredients except the noodles in a blender or food processor, purée and add to casserole. Stir to combine thoroughly and simmer, covered, for 1 hour.

Serve over cooked vermicelli noodles.

Serves 8

André's Chicken Curry

1	chicken
4 Tbsp (50mL)	ghee or clarified butter
1	garlic clove, crushed
1½ tsp (7mL)	coriander
1 tsp (5mL)	chilies
1½ tsp (7mL)	cumin
1 tsp (5mL)	ginger
1 tsp (5mL)	cardamom
½ tsp (2mL)	fenugreek
½ tsp (2mL)	pepper
½ tsp (2mL)	mixed spices
1	onion, finely diced
1	bay leaf
1	cinnamon stick
2½ cups (500mL)	reserved chicken stock
	juice of half a lemon
2 Tbsp (25mL)	red currant jelly
½ cup (50mL)	toasted coconut

Cover chicken with water and simmer in a covered saucepan for 45 minutes. Pour off the stock and reduce it over high heat to 2½ cups (500mL). Remove meat from the bones and set aside.

Heat ghee in a heavy frying pan. Fry garlic and spices for 3 minutes. Add onion and reserved chicken pieces and sauté until brown. Add remaining ingredients except for the coconut and simmer, covered, for 1 hour.

Serve on a bed of rice, topped with coconut.

Serves 4

Pecan Pie

4	eggs
¾ cup (175mL)	sugar
½ tsp (2mL)	salt
1½ cups (375mL)	corn syrup
1 Tbsp (15mL)	melted butter
1 tsp (5mL)	vanilla
2 cups (500mL)	pecan halves
1 9-inch (1-L)	pie crust, unbaked

Preheat oven to 400°F (200°C). Beat eggs lightly. Add sugar, salt, corn syrup, melted butter, and vanilla.

Spread pecans evenly over pie crust. Cover with filling. Place in oven and immediately reduce heat to 350°F (180°C). Bake 45 to 50 minutes or until firm.

Spoonbread

2 cups (500mL)	boiling water
1½ cups (375mL)	cornmeal
1½ tsp (7mL)	salt
2 tsp (10mL)	melted butter
3	eggs, separated
1¼ cups (300mL)	milk

Pour boiling water into a bowl. Sprinkle in cornmeal. Add salt and melted butter and stir well to combine. Set aside so the cornmeal absorbs the liquid and swells.

In a separate bowl beat egg yolks until thick. Gradually add milk. Add to cornmeal mixture.

Beat egg whites until stiff peaks form. Fold into cornmeal mixture. Pour batter into a buttered 2-quart (2-L) casserole or soufflé dish. Bake at 350°F (180°C) for 45 minutes.

Serves 8

Takao Tanabe

When Takao Tanabe, Director of the Banff School of Fine Arts, lived in New York City, he ate repeatedly at a certain Chinese restaurant. They got to know him so well that he was allowed into the kitchen to watch the preparations—as long as he went before five in the afternoon. And there he learned a lot.

"For myself, though, I tend to cook fairly simple things. I eat 'healthy foods'—by that I don't mean 'health foods'—and I have to go to Calgary to buy a lot of the ingredients. I do a lot of stir-fry combinations. The difficult-to-do dishes I save for eating in restaurants.

"I'll eat some superb Japanese dish someplace and think, 'I don't know how to do things like that, but I should.' Somehow, I never get around to learning, though."

Steamed Chicken

1	chicken
	rock salt
	star anise
¼ cup (50mL)	julienne strips of green onion

Dipping Sauce

4 tsp (20mL)	freshly grated ginger root
sprinkling of	coarse salt
¾ cup (175mL)	peanut oil
½ cup (125mL)	soy sauce
4 tsp (20mL)	finely minced green onion

Cut chicken in small serving pieces and discard skin.

Set steamer in wok with about ½ cup (125mL) water in the bottom of the pan. Layer alternately chicken pieces, rock salt, and 2 pieces star anise per piece of meat. Cover and steam for 25 minutes.

To serve, discard anise and salt. Place chicken on platter and spoon some sauce from the bottom of the wok over it. Sprinkle with julienne strips of green onion.

Serve with individual bowls of dipping sauce and rice.

Serves 4

Photo: Charmian Reading

Tony Tascona

It is said that painter, printmaker, and sculptor Tony Tascona is the Master of the Spontaneous Cook-Up. Other Winnipeg artists claim that he always has a pot of chili bubbling on the back burner.

"People are always dropping in. I like my friends to feel welcome at any time. They know they can come over to the house whenever they want and get well fed," says Tony.

"Recently I invited George Swinton, Joe Fafard, Don Proch, and a number of other artists to an outside 'Chili Bean Tascona Cook-Out'— booze and all. They thought it was great. I made a large turkey pan full to the top—and guess what? They scraped the bottom of the pan and the last ones went home at six-thirty in the morning."

It has become the tradition each Christmas for Tony to make the biggest pot possible of his gourmet chili (or a variation of it) and invite all his friends to a tree-trimming party. Everyone brings something to hang on the tree and devours the chili and lots of wine.

Tony tries to keep himself on a low-cholesterol, low-sodium diet, and consequently cooks with very little oil and no salt. Cheese is one of his few weaknesses and he loves to combine it with meat and vegetable dishes.

A large vegetable patch in his backyard yields fresh produce for the family and includes a rather rare (to Winnipeg) type of climbing Jerusalem tomato.

He is a keen salad maker, and each one of his concoctions is a new experience. He never knows until he is finished what might find its way into a salad. It may be lettuce, endives, spinach, carrots, orange, onions, tuna, or salmon, to name but a few of the potential ingredients. For sure, though, there will be basil—it's his favourite herb.

Because Tony cooks most things with a free hand, it is hard to record his recipes. "But you can more or less gauge the amounts of things that would go into what I make," he says.

Gourmet Chili Bean Tascona

2 pounds (1kg)	lean ground beef or ground veal
½ pound (250g)	mushrooms, sliced
1	large onion, chopped
1 cup (250mL)	diced celery
1 14-ounce (398-mL)	can tomato sauce
1 5-ounce (150-mL)	can tomato paste
1 28-ounce (796-mL)	can tomatoes
1 14-ounce (398-mL)	can kidney beans
2 Tbsp (25mL)	chili powder
2	red peppers, diced
1	garlic clove, crushed
2 tsp (10mL)	basil
1 Tbsp (15mL)	brown sugar

Brown the meat in a large casserole. Add mushrooms, onion, and celery, and sauté until tender. Add remaining ingredients, and stir to combine thoroughly.

Cover and simmer for 2 hours, stirring occasionally.

May be served over cooked noodles.

Serves 8

Chicken and Broccoli Casserole

1	boiled chicken
5 cups (750mL)	broccoli florets
1 Tbsp (15mL)	vegetable oil
1	small onion, finely chopped
1	garlic clove, crushed
2 cups (500mL)	grated Mozzarella cheese
½ cup (125mL)	grated Parmesan cheese
1 tsp (5mL)	basil

Remove meat from boiled chicken. Parboil broccoli in boiling salted water for 2 minutes. Drain and refresh under running cold water.

Heat oil in a heavy frying pan. Sauté diced onion and garlic until limp.

Combine cheeses in top of double boiler. Add basil. Heat to melt, stirring constantly. Add onion and garlic. Combine chicken and broccoli in a buttered 2-quart (2-L) casserole. Cover with melted cheese. Bake at 350°F (180°C) for 20 to 30 minutes to heat through.

Serves 4

Zucchini Casserole

1½ cups (375mL)	celery, cut in ½-inch (1-cm) slices
2	large onions, sliced in rings
6	zucchini, cut in ¼-inch (5-mm) slices
3 tsp (15mL)	basil
¾ tsp (3mL)	garlic powder
1 tsp (5mL)	salt
	freshly ground pepper
12 ounces (375g)	Mozzarella cheese, grated

Parboil the celery, onion, and zucchini separately. Drain each and refresh under running cold water.

Combine herbs.

Cover the bottom of a lightly buttered 2-quart (2-L) casserole dish with zucchini slices. Sprinkle with a little of the herb mixture and a thin layer of grated Mozzarella. Alternate a layer of each vegetable with a sprinkling of herbs and Mozzarella. Continue until all ingredients are used, finishing with a layer of cheese. Bake at 350°F (180°C) for 30 minutes.

Serves 8

Omelette à la Tascona

1 Tbsp (15mL)	olive oil
1	garlic clove, crushed
6	eggs, lightly beaten
½ tsp (2mL)	salt
	freshly ground pepper
¼ cup (50mL)	small bread croutons
¼ cup (50mL)	finely diced cooked ham
2 Tbsp (25mL)	finely chopped green onion

Heat oil in a large omelette pan. Sauté garlic until golden. Beat eggs with salt and pepper and pour into pan. Let sit for 30 seconds over medium heat; then tilt pan and lift edges of cooked egg so liquid egg runs underneath. When nearly done, sprinkle with croutons, ham, and green onion.

Fold omelette over and turn out onto a heated plate. Cut into thirds.

Serves 3

Harold Town

"I hate cooking, but I know a lot about it. Just like I detest cards, but I know a lot about them too," says Harold Town. "I'm a superb eater, though. But one dish at a time. I don't want all the food swimming around together on the plate. I'm a purist. I prefer simple, unsauced foods such as a lamb chop or shoulder of spring lamb, which I strongly suspect is the food I like most.

"On the other hand, a meal I adore, but shouldn't because it's part junk, is a creation of the late Albert Franck. You cook some potato and kale and mash it together and top it with lots of fat knackwurst.

"I'll eat anything, but I hate garlic. I consider it the greatest abomination in the world. It masks the real flavour of food. One of my perversions, I suppose, is a patty of ground steak with an egg on top.

"I love fish, barely cooked. I particularly love Malpèque oysters and buy three pecks of them every Christmas. I've been known to consume seventy at one sitting. I'll eat them raw, or perhaps in an oyster stew. They have such a rarefied, exquisite taste."

Harold Town has a house in central Toronto and a farm north of the city that is heaven for anyone who likes to eat. It supports a superb garden of all the standard vegetables as well as such special delights as kale, brown lettuce, salsify, spaghetti squash, and a full range of herbs. The farm has a manager, but Harold says, "I experience a certain macho joy in weeding, and I delight in spreading wood ash around to keep slugs away from my beets."

The farmhouse, now into its second century, comes equipped with an up-to-the-minute walk-in freezer, perfect for storing the bounty of the farm. In addition to fruits and vegetables, the

Photo: Beverley Rockett

Towns raise a miniature United Nations of the fowl kingdom—Polish hens, Chinese geese, Indian ducks and Cornish hens.

Still, Harold Town doesn't cook. "I can't stand anything to do with cooking. I have a psychological aversion to it. It gives me a sore back."

Herb Paste Old Orchard Farm

½ cup (125mL)   olive oil
¼ cup (50mL)   pine nuts
1½ cups (375mL)   fresh herbs—singly or in combination—basil, parsley, marjoram, chives, coriander
2 Tbsp (25mL)   fresh lemon juice
  pinch of salt
  freshly ground pepper

Place all ingredients in container of food processor or blender and pureé until mixture becomes a smooth paste.

Spread on grilled steaks, sautéed fish, or toss with almost any cooked vegetable.

Yield: 1 cup (250mL)

Bangers and Kale à la Albert Franck

4   large potatoes, peeled
3 Tbsp (40mL)   butter
¼ cup (50mL)   milk (approx.)
½ pound (250g)   kale
½ pound (250g)   knackwurst
8   wieners

Boil potatoes until soft, drain, and mash with butter and milk.

Steam kale for about 5 minutes until leaves are just wilted, drain, and squeeze dry. Chop in food processor or with a knife. Combine with mashed potatoes. Spoon into a buttered baking dish.

Boil knackwurst and wieners for 10 minutes. Drain and arrange on top of potatoes. Bake at 350°F (180°C) for 30 minutes or until heated through.

Serves 4

Beets with Cranberry and Orange Sauce

2 pounds (1kg)   baby beets
½ pound (250g)   cranberries
1   orange, cut in eighths

Trim the greens from baby beets leaving ½ inch (1cm) of stalk. Cover with water and simmer until tender—about 35 minutes. Drain. Refresh under running cold water. Slip off skins and remove stem ends. Keep warm.

While beets are cooking, prepare sauce by combining cranberries and orange pieces and chopping finely with a knife or in a food processor fitted with metal blade.

To serve, cut beets in half and toss with sauce.

Serves 8

Irene Whittome

Irene Whittome grew up in Vancouver where she studied art and sculpture. The city's famous Chinese food opened her tastebuds.

"It had to happen somehow, sometime," she laughs. "I endured endless Irish stews when I was a child. It was a family tradition. So to get me interested in food, it had to be something very different from what I was accustomed to and Chinese food did it."

Having lived abroad, Irene has been exposed to many foreign cuisines. "During the six years I lived in Paris, I'd often make couscous just for myself."

Irene, who is a sculptor and who also teaches at Concordia University in Montreal, where she now lives, no longer has much time to work with food as she once did. "I am much more likely to go out to a restaurant with friends than to cook for them.

"I feel a sense of communion in the act of eating. The vibes among people are important, so is the numerology in how many gather together to eat and in what configuration.

"I abhor the way some people simply shovel in food."

Buddha's Feast

1 package	Chinese mushrooms
2 Tbsp (25mL)	black tree fungus
1 pound (500g)	barbecued pork
1	roast duck, Chinese-style with sauce in the cavity
6	garlic cloves
half a	ginger root
1	Chinese green vegetable
1	Chinese cabbage
1 package	Chinese sausages
1 pound (500g)	small squid
2 Tbsp (25mL)	Hoisin sauce
2 Tbsp (25mL)	soy sauce
	sesame oil
	salt and pepper
6 cakes	tofu (bean curd) cut in ½-inch (1-cm) cubes
1 20-ounce (567-g)	can lichees, drained
½ 10-ounce (284-mL)	can water chestnuts, sliced
¼ 6-ounce (170-g)	can pickled ginger, diced
3 3.5-ounce (100-g)	packages Sapporo Ichiban noodles
½ cup (125mL)	toasted sesame seeds

Soak Chinese mushrooms and tree fungus in hot water for 30 minutes. Drain and set aside.

Set pork and duck, cut into small pieces, on separate platters ready to use.

Slice garlic and ginger root into very thin slivers. Set aside.

Cut Chinese green vegetable and cabbage in 1½-inch (4-cm) pieces. Set aside.

Cut Chinese sausages on the diagonal in ¼-inch (5-mm) pieces. Steam for 10 minutes. Set aside.

Split squid down the length of their bodies. Remove and discard the jelly. Wash and dry squid, then cut in diamond shapes. Set aside.

Prepare sauce by heating together Hoisin sauce, soy sauce, and 1 cup (250mL) of the sauce from inside the duck. Set aside.

Heat a little sesame oil in a large wok. Add a little of the ginger and garlic and the squid. Sauté until the edges of the squid curl, sprinkle with salt and pepper, remove to a platter, and keep warm.

Add more sesame oil to wok and a little more ginger and garlic.

Add bean curd, pork, and duck, and sauté until curd is browned; then add remaining sauce from inside the duck. Add drained lichees. When heated through, remove all to a platter and keep warm.

Re-oil the wok. Add ginger, garlic, and green vegetables. Cover and steam for about 5 minutes or until greens are warm and tender but not soft. Stir occasionally.

Combine all ingredients together including the meats and vegetables, water chestnuts, and pickled ginger. Heat through for 7 to 10 minutes during which time the noodles should be cooking in boiling water. Drain them and spread on a large platter. Top with a mound of the meat and vegetable combination. Sprinkle with toasted sesame seeds.

Serves 12

Index

207